A Simplified Chart

ra
aina

2)
— m. Yolande-Irene   Eudokia   other
    of Montferrat   children

John   Teodoro   Demetrios   Simonis - m. Milutin
     of Montferrat   of Serbia

JOHN VI ——— m. Irene
KANTAKOUZENOS | Asen

na   Matthias   other   Theodora - m. Sultan
kouzene   children   Orkhan

na   Theodore I   Michael
gases   of the Morea

Andronikos   CONSTANTINE   Demetrios   Thomas
                   XI
              m. 1. Magdalena
                  Tocco
              2 Catarina
              Gattilusi

Imperial
Twilight

Imperial
Twilight
The Palaiologos Dynasty

and the
Decline of Byzantium

Constance Head

nh Nelson-Hall
Chicago

Library of Congress Cataloging in Publication Data

Head, Constance.
   Imperial twilight.

   Bibliography: p.
   Includes index.
   1. Palaeologi, House of. 2. Byzantine
Empire—History. I. Title.
DF631.H4   949.5'04   76–26527
ISBN 0–88229–368–0

Manufactured in the United States of America

Contents

Acknowledgments

Imperial Twilight was partially written during the year when I held a Younger Humanists Fellowship from the National Endowment for the Humanities. For that period of uninterrupted study, I am deeply grateful to the Endowment.

I wish to express gratitude, too, to the following individuals and institutions who assisted in various ways in the completion of the book:

To Professor John W. Barker of the University of Wisconsin who read an earlier draft of the manuscript and made many helpful suggestions for its improvement.

To the Interlibrary Loan staff at Western Carolina University and particularly to Joan K. Lesueur, for diligent searching for hard-to-find materials.

To Audrey Clayton for her dedicated and very accurate typing of the manuscript.

To my literary agent, James Allen.

To my aunt, Helen Thompson, who read the manuscript and offered much encouragement.

To the editors of *Mankind* for permission to incorporate parts of my article, "Manuel Palaiologos, The Traveling Emperor" (*Mankind*, IV, no. 3, October, 1973), in this work.

To the Graduate School at Western Carolina University for a Research Grant to facilitate completion of the manuscript.

And very special thanks to my mother, who was my best encourager in the days when I pursued the fortunes of the Palaiologos family.

1

Introduction

This is the story of a family, the House of Palaiologos, the longest-lived and last of the reigning dynasties of imperial Byzantium. The Palaiologoi ruled for almost two hundred years, from 1259 to 1453. Their empire, though a land of great and ancient traditions, was throughout these last two centuries of its existence a nation struggling for survival, surrounded by enemies outside and torn by factionalism within.

The generations between the crafty, terrible Michael VIII, founder of the family, and Constantine XI, the last heroic defender of the dying empire, present a wide gallery of personalities. Beneath the strange hemispherical crown of Byzantium adorned with cascading strings of jewels, the ten Palaiologan emperors are distinctive individuals, men whose plans and ambitions, for good or ill, would mold forever the future of their country.

The Byzantine Empire, the great medieval continuator of the ancient Roman state, still remains an unfamiliar land to many readers of history. The medieval Byzantines were Greek-speakers (*Palaiologos*, incidentally, is a Greek name meaning "ancient word"). The imperial tradition, however, goes back to Rome and to Constantine the

Great, the fourth-century Roman emperor who established the city of Constantinople and made it his capital in A.D. 330. Out of that move the Roman Empire of the East—the Byzantine Empire—was born. Through the centuries, long after the city of Rome had passed into other hands, the Byzantines would continue to speak of themselves as "Romans." And even when their territories were confined to scattered sections of Asia Minor, Greece, and the Balkans—indeed, even when at the last there was nothing left but Constantinople itself—their sovereign was officially titled Emperor—*Basileus* and *Autokrator*—of the Romans.

The Palaiologoi proudly displayed the device of the "Roman" eagle, though in fact this symbol bore little resemblance to its prototype, the eagles of the ancient Roman legions. The later Byzantine version was a creature with two heads, that it might "look East and West," and with the Greek letters ΠΑΛΓ (for *Palaiologos*) often emblazoned on its breast in a curious design. It was the same sort of logic that saw in this fabulous creature a Roman eagle that could view Constantinople itself as "New Rome."

The Byzantines loved Constantinople with a mighty passion; it was the "city of all cities." Once, long before the Palaiologoi ruled, it had been the largest city of the Christian world, and if time and misfortune had robbed it of much of its former beauty and wealth, it was even in the last centuries of the empire the hub upon which all else depended.

The Palaiologoi and their subjects could not forget how in former centuries Byzantium had ranked among the most important world powers. In the early Middle Ages, in fact, the empire was indisputably the strongest, wealthiest, and most cultured state in Christendom. But that was long ago, before the nomadic Turks came riding out of the steppes of central Asia to carve out a homeland for themselves in territories that had once been Byzantium's finest provinces. It was in the eleventh century that the first Turkish tribes came into Asia Minor in great numbers. Two hundred years later, when Michael, the first of the Palaiologan emperors, was born, the Turks were still there, fervent followers of Islam and perennial enemies of the Orthodox Christian Byzantines.

But if the Turks were a foe to be feared, so also were the "Latin" Christians of Western Europe. While story-tellers of the West chronicled the glorious deeds of the Crusaders, Byzantines looked back to the successive waves of these "soldiers of God" as marking a terrible time in their history. "Crusaders" who apparently believed Greek Orthodox Christians were no better than infidels, who slaughtered and plundered indiscriminately, and who at length in 1204 captured Constantinople itself—these were a worse foe than the Turks had ever been! Many a Byzantine held this opinion, and with ample justification.

For more than half a century after the terrible year 1204, a line of "Latin" emperors (really Belgians, but the Byzantines described everyone from Western Europe as "Latins") ruled in Constantinople, their shaky throne heavily supported by the merchant republic of Venice. As an aftermath of the "crusade," semi-independent Latin principalities were established in various parts of the Greek world. Meanwhile the Byzantine imperial court moved across the Straits of the Bosphoros to Nicaea, about forty miles from the old imperial capital.

At the outset, Nicaea's position as headquarters for the "empire-in-exile" was anything but secure. Not only was a large part of the old Byzantine Empire in the hands of the Venetians and other "Latins," but there emerged also a rival Greek state, the Despotate of Epiros on the Adriatic coast that refused to recognize Nicaea's claim. In spite of these problems, the emperors of the Laskaris-Vatatzes dynasty in Nicaea never ceased to believe that their location there was a "temporary" move or to abandon hope of dislodging the crusader emperors and their Venetian allies from Constantinople. Fifty-seven years were to pass before this goal was accomplished, but at last in 1261, the deed was done; the imperial city returned to Byzantine hands, and the Palaiologos dynasty in the person of Michael VIII ascended the ancient throne of the emperors in Constantinople.

How the shattered Empire of Byzantium came to regain the lost capital and to experience a new lease on life in the late thirteenth century is, however, only the beginning of the Palaiologan story. Subsequent generations witnessed the gradual fading of this reborn empire, as Michael VIII's descendants faced new problems both from outside their borders and within their midst, and the tide of history rolled inevitably on toward the final fall of Constantinople to the Ottoman Turks in 1453.

Though there are a number of excellent, highly specialized monographs on various facets of the Palaiologan epoch, there is still relatively little available in the way of general studies of the period as a whole beyond the summary treatments included in larger Byzantine histories. I present this volume with the object of partially filling the need for such introductory material, and it is my hope that through this series of personal glimpses of the Palaiologan emperors and the time in which they lived, the intelligent layman or student of history will come to sense more vividly the nature of the long-vanished Byzantine world in its last tragic yet glorious years of imperial twilight.

2

Prelude to Power

His subjects called him John the Merciful. By the midthirteenth century, when he had already reigned for thirty years and more, he was an institution in the Empire of Nicaea: a frail, dark, aging little man whose blood connection with earlier Byzantine royalty was remote to say the least, but whose abilities both as a militarist and as an administrator amply justified his claim to rule. John Doukas Vatatzes was a benevolent and much-loved emperor; under his guidance the Byzantine "government in exile" had been transformed from an insecure string of fortresses in Asia Minor into a strong bloc of reconquered territories on both the European and Asiatic sides of the Bosphoros. True, the crusader lords and their Venetian collaborators still held Constantinople, the old Byzantine capital, and had resisted all of Vatatzes' efforts to dislodge them. The emperor, now growing old and increasingly disabled by severe attacks of epilepsy, must have realized that the glory of regaining the capital city—if ever such glory came about—would belong to another.

He must have realized, too, that however popular he was with the common folk who lived under his rule, his own court was a hotbed of intrigue—plots that loomed the more dangerous because his heir, his only son, Theodore, was an unhealthy, neurotic, ill-tempered young man, a veritable magnet for trouble. There were sure to be others, closer kin to the old imperial line who had ruled in the centuries of Byzantium's glory, who would imagine themselves better qualified than Theodore for the crown.

Such a man was Michael Doukas Angelos Komnenos Palaiologos: a bold and dashing young military officer whose very name proclaimed openly his kinship with three of the great imperial families of Byzantium's past. Michael's mother claimed direct descent from several of the earlier emperors, including the great Alexios Komnenos, to whom practically every aspirant to the Byzantine crown for generations traced his family tree. Michael's father, the Grand Domestic Andronikos Palaiologos, was slightly less nobly born, but the Palaiologoi were an ancient and famous family. They boasted descent from Alexios Komnenos' brother-in-law George Palaiologos, a famous general and military hero of the late eleventh century. Perhaps young Michael had always resented the fact that he who could claim descent from such a host of distinguished ancestors had to serve an upstart with practically no imperial background. Though the Emperor John Doukas Vatatzes professed intense pride in the name of Doukas, his kinship with the emperors of that dynasty—if authentic at all—was extremely remote.[1] John Vatatzes wore the Byzantine crown because in his youth he had married the heiress to the throne, Princess Irene Laskaris. It was as simple at that: without Irene, who was by now long dead, Vatatzes would have been a nobody.

There were some who whispered, too, that the imperial aspirations supposedly harbored by Michael Palaiologos might at least in part be traced back to his early childhood. When he was a mere baby, it was said, his older sister, Eulogia, often rocked him to sleep with a lullaby which promised he would someday become the basileus and would "enter Constantinople through the

Golden Gate," the gate reserved for imperial triumphal processions.[2] Michael's mother, it seems, died young, and the boy was reared by Eulogia and another older sister, Martha.[3] Whether or not the two girls really filled the mind of their little brother with imperial dreams is impossible to say, but in any event, Eulogia's lullaby in time was to prove singularly prophetic.

As befitted a nobly born youth, when he was still a young boy, Michael was sent to live at the palace of the Emperor John Vatatzes. The court of the Byzantine Empire-in-exile was a center of learning and scholarly activity, and Michael received an excellent education, perhaps together with John Vatatzes' son, the heir to the throne, Prince Theodore, who was almost exactly his age. Years later, Michael wrote that the Emperor Vatatzes treated him as if he were his own son,[4] but significantly in the few scattered autobiographical notes he left behind him, Michael tends to ignore the unpleasant reality of Theodore's existence almost altogether. The young men were clearly not friends. Theodore was bookish; he wrote theological treatises and incomprehensible discourses, while Michael, strong and athletic, seemed born to be a soldier.

Because of his noble connections, Michael obtained a commission as a matter of course. By the time he was in his midtwenties, it was generally agreed that he was an extremely useful if potentially dangerous young officer, as gifted in the fine art of intrigue as in actual combat.

Against this background, in the autumn of 1253, confused and disturbing reports began to reach the ears of the old Emperor Vatatzes. Michael, who was by this time the military governor of the Thracian towns of Melnik and Serres, was plotting something most unsavory—perhaps against the emperor's life. Vatatzes evidently believed him guilty and decided his fate (with a severity most unusual for "John the Merciful"). Let the accused be put to trial: not according to the ancient practices of Roman law, cherished by the Byzantines through the centuries, but by the new method lately introduced by the Latin crusaders from Western Europe, the ordeal of the red-hot iron. The venerable Bishop Phokas of the town of Philadelphia in Asia Minor was sent to conduct the proceedings. To prove his innocence, Michael would have to pick up a piece of iron, heated red hot for this purpose. If he could do so without burning his hand, it would be deemed a miracle—and a sign he was not guilty.

It was a tense moment. Before a large crowd of witnesses, most of whom were apparently sympathetic to the accused, Michael Palaiologos turned calmly to face Bishop Phokas. "I am not such a one as to perform miracles," he said. "If a red-hot iron should fall upon the hand of a living man, I do not doubt that it would burn him." But, he added, if the bishop would care to lift the hot iron himself and hand it to him, he would accept it.[5]

The crowd gasped—and Bishop Phokas declined Michael's suggestion. The young man's cool mockery of the barbaric custom broke up the trial, and Phokas had no option but to send a report of his failure to John Doukas Vatatzes.

Fortunately for Michael (if unfortunately for Vatatzes' descendants), the old emperor seems to have found the entire incident highly amusing. Michael Palaiologos, clever, quick-witted, and fearless, was entirely too valuable a man to destroy, regardless of what he might have done in the past. The charges were dropped, and Michael was instead rewarded with an imperial bride, Vatatzes' grandniece, Theodora Doukaina. The marriage would be a stormy one, with much infidelity on Michael's part, and at least once in the years to come he would threaten to divorce her for a more advantageous alliance. Theodora, however, proved devoted to her difficult husband. Contrary to the usual custom which dictated that Byzantine ladies should retain their own surnames, she promptly adopted her husband's name in its feminine form, and henceforth was known as Theodora Doukaina Palaiologina.[6] It was a precedent that many Byzantine women would follow in the years to come.

Newly married to his aristocratic bride, Michael had a future which seemed secure. Just about a year later, however, in 1254, the Emperor John Doukas Vatatzes suffered a fatal epileptic seizure while strolling in his garden. His son Theodore, by the custom of hereditary succession, was unquestionably heir to the throne. However unsuited he may have been for the position of rulership, he succeeded without incident as the Emperor Theodore II.

Incidentally, much to the confusion of modern readers, Theodore had chosen to be called by his mother's surname, Laskaris, rather than his father's; this was a perfectly acceptable though infrequent practice in the Byzantine world, and implied no slur whatsoever on Vatatzes' memory. The reasons for Theodore's preference are not clear. Perhaps he simply felt that "Laskaris" carried with it an imperial aura that was lacking in "Vatatzes," since the latter was derived from a Greek word meaning "bramble bush" and was the subject of numerous puns.

But if Theodore had refused to take his father's name, he had in him nonetheless one undeniable heritage from John Vatatzes: he was an epileptic. While the old Emperor John had for years ruled ably in spite of his handicap, Theodore, who may well have had the disease in a more severe form, was in any event more inclined to dwell morbidly on his affliction. Moody and suspicious, Theodore Laskaris was a difficult master to serve.

Michael Palaiologos, who was after all almost certainly guilty of imperial aspirations, must have felt himself caught in a hopeless situation. The vengeful new emperor, he confessed to a close friend, the historian George Akropolites, seemed much inclined to have him arrested and possibly blinded.[7] This horrible practice, it must be noted, was all too common in the medieval world; the Byzantines were probably no more prone than either their Latin or their Turkish neighbors to inflict the penalty of blinding upon offenders. It was simply accepted as a stern but necessary reality of life by men of those times. Michael, of course, had no inclination to risk the loss of his own eyesight, and thus decided to put himself beyond Theodore's reach. With a few devoted and equally daring companions, he crossed the Turkish frontier and volunteered for service in the Turkish army. The Seljuk sultan, informed of the acquisition of this most unlikely recruit, promptly placed thirty-year-old Michael in command of a troop of Christian mercenaries.

It is not difficult to imagine the wrath of the Emperor Theodore when he learned where Michael had gone, though perhaps too he felt a certain measure of relief at being rid of an ambitious rival. In any event, for almost three years, Michael Palaiologos fought for the Turks in campaigns against their enemies farther to the east, the Mongols.

Meanwhile in the Byzantine realm, Theodore's physical maladies grew progressively worse. "The suffering I experience is insupportable," he wrote. "The doctors do nothing and prate only nonsense."[8] The severity of his illness did not improve Theodore's disposition. He was morbidly suspicious that unknown enemies were working magic against him, a fear that made the lives of those around him constantly insecure.[9]

Yet strangely enough, Theodore Laskaris was a capable soldier. As if determined to defy the limitations of his frail body, he assumed personal command of his troops and endured the hardships of rigorous campaigning and forced marches through wretched winter weather with remarkable stamina. The Byzantines of Nicaea faced new threats to the security of their empire-in-exile now that Vatatzes was dead, and Theodore's short reign, as it turned out, would be spent in an almost constant series of struggles against these foes.

In spite of the long and diligent attempts of Vatatzes to

bring all the Greek-speaking inhabitants of the former imperial territories under his sway, there were still areas which refused to acknowledge the Nicaean government. The most formidable of these was the Despotate of Epiros along the Adriatic coast northwest of Greece, which stubbornly maintained itself as an independent principality with a line of princes of its own. From time to time, the despotate warred against the Byzantines of Nicaea. It was against these Epirote Greeks that Theodore Laskaris would direct most of his military efforts.[10]

Meanwhile the Seljuk Turks, who had long been considered among the Byzantines' deadliest enemies and who had given refuge to the fugitive Michael, were being increasingly hard pressed by the Mongols of Central Asia. In desperation, the Seljuk sultan opened negotiations for an alliance with Theodore; with the provision that Michael Palaiologos be returned to his own people, Theodore agreed. Thus after nearly three years as an officer in the Turkish army, Michael was compelled to return to the court of Nicaea. He must have had grave qualms concerning his future, and according to some accounts, he appeared before the Emperor Theodore clad in penitential sackcloth and ashes.

Theodore at first seemed inclined to forgive and forget. Michael agreed to swear an oath of eternal loyalty to the Laskaris family. In return he was restored to his previous rank in the Byzantine army, immediately assigned command of a small force which included some Turkish mercenaries, and dispatched to Thessaloniki to assist in the struggle against Epiros.

Those who served Theodore Laskaris soon realized, however, how rapidly one's fortunes might change with the whim of the unpredictable emperor. Not long after his official pardon, Michael was summoned to return to the imperial court and without benefit of trial was thrown into prison on the suspicion of disloyalty. Then, a few weeks later, he was informed that he might once again have his freedom if he would renew his oath of eternal loyalty to the house of Laskaris: Theodore and his little son John.[11] Michael swore readily and, we may suppose, with enthusiasm; he was always an excellent actor. A loyalty oath was completely meaningless to him. Once again he was reinstated in his military command.

Not long thereafter, in August 1258, Theodore Laskaris died and was buried in the monastery of Sosandra beside his father, John Doukas Vatatzes. The new basileus, Theodore's only son, John IV, was about eight or nine years old. The child's mother, Helen Asen, had died several years earlier, and so according to the terms of Theodore's will, the regency was bestowed upon George Muzalon, who held the rank of *protovestarios* and who had been the late emperor's best friend. It was not a wise appointment. Muzalon was sadly lacking in the two attributes that might have won him the support of his contemporaries: noble birth and military prestige.

The period of mourning for the dead Theodore was not even over when a group of malcontents, almost certainly at the instigation of Michael Palaiologos, contrived a plot to send the new regent to join his late friend and sovereign.[12] The conspirators chose to act while Muzalon was attending a memorial service for Theodore at Sosandra. A large crowd of civilian rabble and soldiers, including a considerable number of Latin mercenaries, surrounded the monastery where the service was being held, brandishing weapons and shouting for the little Emperor John to appear. The boy was brought out before his subjects; his guards, who apparently were party to the plot, instructed him to make a signal for quiet. The frightened child waved his hands energetically at the mob, not realizing that the soldiers were determined to interpret his "signal" as an appeal for action. Unrestrained they burst into the monastery. The liturgy stopped abruptly and a scuffle followed. George Muzalon and his brother scurried for hiding places, while a conspirator stabbed one of Muzalon's aides in the back, professing to have mistaken him for the Regent George. The noble ladies present were screaming and crying; and George Muzalon's wife ran to Michael Palaiologos, who was her uncle, and pleaded with him to do something. Michael's reply indicated only too clearly the depth of his involvement. "Be quiet, woman, or you may be next!" he warned in effect.[13]

Meanwhile the regent and his brother were dragged from their hiding places; one was behind a door, the other under the altar. George, indisputably identified by the green shoes that were the sign of his rank, pleaded for mercy and offered to pay a large ransom, but the conspirators were merciless. The Muzalon brothers were slain on the spot. In gross violation of the ancient laws of sanctuary, the nine-day regency of George Muzalon had ended. The reign of Michael Doukas Angelos Komnenos Palaiologos—the Emperor Michael VIII—was about to begin.

3

Michael the Crafty

In the weeks that followed Muzalon's death, Michael assumed the titles of Grand Duke and Despot. His assertion of a claim to the imperial crown, everyone realized, was simply a matter of time. Perhaps the only dignitary of the Nicaean court with any genuine concern for the child emperor, John Laskaris, was Arsenios, the stern and devout old monk whom Theodore had appointed patriarch. As the spiritual head of Greek Orthodoxy, Arsenios was able to argue vigorously in behalf of the boy emperor's rights, but at length, realizing that there was nothing he could do to stop the ambitious Michael, he decided to make common cause with him. Perhaps he might convince him at least not to harm the child. After all, it had been a frequent custom in earlier centuries to install a senior partner as co-emperor when the legitimate heir was a child. In most cases this arrangement had worked surprisingly well. Arsenios hoped for the best, extorted assurances from Michael that he would never forget he was merely a deputy for young John, and by December of 1258, announced he was willing to perform a joint coronation.

There is no hint as to what John Laskaris thought of his newly acquired co-emperor. Michael, however, we can be sure, had no warm spot in his heart at all for John. The boy was simply a reminder of the detestable Emperor Theodore and an obstacle to the establishment of a Palaiologos dynasty. Although Michael and his wife Theodora had no sons of their own as yet, the ambitious co-emperor was already dreaming of the day when the Palaiologoi would replace the Laskarids forever.

The stories told of Michael's abominable behavior at his own coronation may reflect as much gossip as fact. They are, however, indicative of the future course of events. Michael, it seems, had promised the Patriarch Arsenios that the boy John should be crowned *first;* then during the ceremonies, he suddenly demanded the right of precedence for himself and his wife. The terrified Arsenios knew all too well that Michael commanded the loyalties of the many soldiers who were present. He had no choice but to obey.[1] Moreover, young John, perhaps acting on instructions from Michael, added his comment that he would rather not be crowned at all if only Michael would keep him safe. Thus Michael and his Empress Theodora received their crowns with due solemnity, while it is unclear if John had any proper coronation at all. When the services were over that day, the boy who was emperor by right of birth was seen leaving the church wearing a small circlet of pearls and walking some paces behind Michael Palaiologos, who wore the official imperial diadem. John was, however, undoubtedly recognized as emperor, if very much the junior partner, and for the next few years official documents were issued in the names of Michael and John together.

During this time, Michael devoted his energies principally to military matters. The ongoing struggle with Epiros and the long-range goal of reconquest of Constantinople both demanded his attention. Ironically, although Michael was an excellent soldier, he was never personally present for any of the greatest victories of his reign. At the battle of Pelagonia in 1259, Byzantine forces under command of Michael's brother inflicted a heavy defeat upon a league of the allies of the Despotate of Epiros.

With these foes subdued, Michael's plans for Constantinople moved ahead rapidly. While he negotiated a truce with the weak, ineffectual Baldwin II de Courtenay, who currently wore the crown of the so-called Latin Empire of Constantinople, Michael was at the same time deep in negotiations with the Italian Republic of Genoa. The Genoese were the fiercest rivals of the Venetians, and it was Venetian support alone that maintained Baldwin on his shaky throne. In return for the support of the Genoese navy, Michael promised that when Constantinople was his, Genoa should enjoy all the commercial advantages that Venice now held under Baldwin, including the right to trade duty-free anywhere in the empire. Early in 1261, the secret treaty of Nymphaion was signed by Genoese authorities and by the Emperor Michael. They had now only to wait until Michael's truce with Baldwin ran out in the summer of the same year.[2] In the meantime, Byzantine reconnaissance forces infiltrated the areas near Constantinople and discovered that many of Baldwin's Greek-speaking rural subjects were ready to help restore Constantinople to Greek rule.

It is uncertain how deeply Michael was personally involved in the intrigues that brought down Baldwin's throne. In any event, he was not present when Constantinople fell into Byzantine hands. It was mid-July of 1261, and Michael was encamped with a portion of his army at Meterion about two hundred miles from Constantinople, when early one morning his sister Eulogia entered his tent with the important tidings. Not wishing to startle him too suddenly, Eulogia, we are informed, tickled her brother's toes until he awoke; then announced her great news: "Emperor, you are master of Constantinople."

"How can I be when I am in Meterion?" asked the scarcely awakened Michael, to which Eulogia replied piously, "Christ has granted you Constantinople," and then proceeded to explain what had happened.[3] A reconnaissance expedition under command of General Alexios Strategopoulos had gotten wind of the surprising fact that the capital was practically defenseless. The Venetian fleet was absent, engaged in an attack on Daphnusia on the Black Sea, and with the fleet were almost all of the Latin emperor's troops. Pro-Byzantine collaborators inside the city offered to open a gate to Strategopoulos' forces. It was an opportunity entirely too good to be missed; of course, the truce between Michael and Baldwin had not yet expired, but Strategopoulos knew his master well enough to be sure that he would agree that truces were made to be broken. The plan worked perfectly. Constantinople, after fifty-seven years of Latin rule, returned to the hands of the Byzantines in a practically bloodless victory. Numerous Latins fled for their lives, including the Emperor Baldwin II, who sailed away on one of the few Venetian ships remaining in the harbor. He departed so hastily that he left his crown and sword behind him in the imperial palace.

After all of Michael's careful planning, the Genoese had not been needed after all. There would be time enough later on to worry about whether they could compel him to carry out the terms of the treaty of Nymphaion. Michael's interests for the present centered upon his ceremonial entry into Constantinople.

On the fifteenth of August 1261, the Emperor Michael Palaiologos entered the regained capital through the Golden Gate. With a display of Byzantine pageantry and piety calculated to delight the hearts of the city's inhabitants, the ancient and very holy icon of the Hodegetria—Our Lady of the Way—reputedly painted by St. Luke, was paraded through the streets, while Michael followed humbly on foot, as if to acknowledge that he owed his victory solely to the assistance of the Blessed Virgin. The crowds cheered enthusiastically as the emperor—dark-haired, young and strong, the very prototype of Byzantium's ancient glories—walked in their midst.

Michael, for his part, saw that the city of his dreams was a shambles: dirty, desolate, underpopulated, and poor. As the historian Gregoras reported, the city "had received no care from the Latins, except destruction of every kind day and night."⁴ The churches which before the half-century of Latin rule had held countless precious relics, were plundered of their treasures; Blachernai Palace, in the northwest corner of the city, once by far the loveliest of the imperial residences, was practically in ruins. The wretched Baldwin had stripped the lead off the roof to be melted down for coinage, while the interior was grimy, blackened by "Italian smoke."⁵ Michael, his family, and his court installed themselves in the scarcely more habitable Great Palace at the eastern end of the city near the Bosphoros.

Within a short time the work of rebuilding the ruined city began. Michael's soldiers were set to work on the construction of public buildings, market places, law courts, theaters, and homes for the aged. The roofs of many of the city's churches, like that of Blachernai Palace, had been stripped of their lead, and Michael, who knew that piety was good politics in Byzantium, was particularly concerned for their restoration. Outside the great Church of the Holy Apostles, burial place of many of the earlier emperors, he ordered the erection of a monumental column in honor of his patron saint, Michael the Archangel. A statue of St. Michael stood atop the column, while at its base was a statue of Michael Palaiologos the Emperor, holding up a model of the city as an offering to his heavenly patron.⁶

It was soon clear that the lavish rebuilding schemes of the emperor would demand far greater financial resources than he had at hand. Michael made a genuine effort to return land holdings confiscated from the defeated Latins to descendants of the families who had held the properties in 1204. Of course, he expected generous "contributions" from the individuals whose family fortunes were thus restored. But "voluntary donations" of this sort fell far short of the vast sums needed in rebuilding the city. Taxes were increased sharply; the people grumbled and began to feel nostalgia for the good old days of Baldwin de Courtenay.

Michael's popularity suffered a further blow when it was learned what had happened to John Laskaris, who was after all still the rightful emperor. Sometime in the winter of 1261, on Christmas Day according to some reports, Michael ordered the unfortunate boy to be blinded. The process employed was supposed to be the most "merciful" of several methods in use at the time: little John, who was now about eleven or twelve years old, was forced to stare at an intense concentration of light until his sight was destroyed. The boy was then whisked off to the desolate fortress of Dacybyza on the coast of the Black Sea, where he was sentenced to life imprisonment.[7]

The unprecedented cruelty of Michael's dealing with the defenseless child came as a shock even in a milieu where "judicial mutilation" of adult offenders was an accepted practice. There is a possibility that the injury to the child's eyesight was not permanent; years later, reports (which were never conclusively proven) circulated to the effect that John Laskaris, now a grown man and no longer blind, had escaped to Sicily.[8] Certainly in many cases, blinding by light concentration produced only temporary loss of eyesight, and one may hope that in John's case these rumors were true. Nevertheless, it seems more likely that John Laskaris remained blind and imprisoned forever. One Russian source lists him as a saint, indicating that he grew resigned to his fate and lived a life of patient and pious resignation.[9]

In any case, there is no doubt of the penalty Michael *intended* for John Laskaris. The Patriarch Arsenios, who had been powerless to protect young John, could at least speak out fearlessly on the dreadful wrong that had been done. In solemn ceremony he pronounced the excommunication of the Emperor Michael.

Michael reciprocated by deposing the patriarch, but it was not until many months later that he found a compliant priest ready to lift the excommunication in return for promotion to the patriarchal throne. One suspects that excommunication made little difference to the emperor personally, but some effort had to be made to conciliate public opinion.

While Michael thus intrigued to salvage his sinking popularity at home, he was also constantly involved in schemes to protect his empire from external enemies. Whatever one may think of him as a person, Michael was undoubtedly a brilliant statesman. His long reign, as it turned out, would involve a continuous struggle for the reborn empire's survival. Byzantium was surrounded by enemy states. In the East lay the realms of the Seljuk Turks; in the West, the weakened but still hostile Despotate of Epiros and the crusader principality of Achaia in Greece. An additional enemy was Bulgaria, whose king had married a sister of little John Laskaris. Further away, but potentially most dangerous of all, was the wealthy and powerful Kingdom of Sicily. Under King Manfred and then under his successor, the scheming French lord, Charles of Anjou, Sicily would prove Michael's bitterest foe.

While it would be extraneous here to trace in detail the varied diplomatic and military moves of the first Palaiologos emperor, the outstanding characteristics of Michael's foreign policy are worth noting. To neutralize the danger of his nearer foes, Michael was always ready to make alliances with powers further away. Hungary, a traditional enemy of the Bulgars, was brought into Michael's network of alliances when the emperor agreed to receive a Hungarian princess, Anna, as a bride for his son and heir, Andronikos. While legitimate "purple-born" imperial children could not be married off to "infidels,"

Michael, fortunately for his international schemes, had two illegitimate daughters. One of these he sent to the Mongol leader, Ilkhan Abagha; the other to Nogai, a Tartar chieftain. These Eastern potentates were to serve as a check on the ambitions of the Seljuk sultan whose land bordered those of the Byzantines in Asia Minor.

To the Genoese, with whom he had originally allied in the treaty of Nymphaion, Michael, somewhat reluctantly true to his word, granted the trading privileges specified in the treaty and in addition the outpost of Pera (or Galata as it was sometimes called) straight across the Golden Horn from Constantinople itself. In return for these favors, they remained Michael's allies against Venice.

Useful as this network of alliances was to Byzantium, Michael soon discovered that something more was needed in order to forestall the intrigues of his greatest enemy, the Sicilian monarch Charles of Anjou.[10] Charles was intensely ambitious; a brother of the French King St. Louis, he had obtained papal approval for his plan to wrest the crown of Sicily from its illegitimate holder, Manfred of Hohenstaufen. Having successfully vanquished Manfred, Charles turned to schemes of further aggrandizement. An alliance with the fallen Emperor Baldwin de Courtenay (Baldwin's son married Charles' daughter) gave him the pretext he needed for designs against Constantinople. Other allies included lords of the crusader principalities of Greece which Michael had not been able to bring back under Byzantine rule. For some years it was open knowledge that Charles was planning a new "crusade" to dethrone "the usurper Palaiologos."

Michael realized clearly that to stall this aggressor, he must counter by winning the friendship of the most prestigious power of Western Europe, the only power which might be able to hold the ambitious Charles in check: the papacy. The emperor, to whom matters of religion mattered little personally, knew also that in negotiations with the papacy, Byzantium possessed a certain advantage: the prospect of uniting the Eastern Orthodox with the Roman Catholic Church. The official schism between the two branches of Christianity dated back to 1054 when a Catholic cardinal had excommunicated the Orthodox patriarch of Constantinople. The suspicion and ill will between the churches of East and West went back many centuries earlier, and were rooted at least as much in cultural and ethnic differences as in any matters of dogma. Most of all, the fifty-seven years when the Latins occupied Constantinople had intensified East-West hatreds. Yet Michael Palaiologos could never understand the reluctance of the Byzantines to accept reunion of the churches; from the purely political viewpoint such union was to Byzantium's advantage in every way. As long as there was a possibility that the Empire of the East might "return" to the Catholic fold, the pope would refuse to bless Charles of Anjou's proposed "crusade" against Byzantium. So Michael reasoned, and so for a number of years he was able to prolong negotiations and to forestall the imperialistic schemes of the King of Sicily.

When finally Pope Gregory X became insistent that the reunion actually be implemented, Michael, still counting on political advantage, was willing to comply. In 1274, envoys including the historian Akropolites were sent to the pope's council in France, and there assented to the Union of Lyons. The schism between the two branches of Christendom supposedly was ended; the Orthodox had recognized papal supremacy.

As his descendants would rediscover many times in the next two centuries, however, there was more to healing the schism than the signing of documents. For the vast majority of Byzantines, no political advantage was worth the price of union with the papacy. It was from the lands of the Latin West that Byzantium's worst enemies had come in the past, and no agreements concluded by the emperor's representatives in far-away Lyons could wipe away the long memories of East-West hostility. In the opinion of most of his people, the Emperor Michael Palaiologos was a traitor to his faith.

With all the ruthlessness of which he was capable, Michael set about to make the union a reality. The results were disastrous. The more he persecuted, the more his subjects defied him, ready to submit to torture and death for their Orthodox faith. As the number of victims grew, even Michael's sister Eulogia, who had always been among his staunchest supporters, turned against him and removed herself to Bulgaria with the openly avowed intention of doing all in her power to undermine her brother's position.[11]

But worst of all for Michael were developments in Rome. Though for several years after the Union of Lyons the papacy proved a loyal ally, the situation altered radically when a Frenchman, Martin IV, was chosen pope in 1281. Martin was wholly in sympathy with the empire-building schemes of Charles of Anjou and willing to give Charles the papal blessing he needed to undertake the conquest of Byzantium. The pope's inclinations were made amply clear to Michael when he received a papal bull, proclaiming him excommunicated for having failed to implement the union![12]

It was now only a matter of time, Michael knew, before King Charles would launch his great "crusade."

In all his struggles to preserve the empire, Michael had relied as much upon diplomacy as upon military force. The best way to stop Charles, he clearly realized, would be by stirring up a situation that would prohibit his leaving Sicily. The Sicilian people, Michael knew, had little love for their French sovereign. The island kingdom was a potential seedbed of revolt.

Throughout the months of 1281, Michael's secret agents were at work in Sicily, generously distributing Byzantine gold. At the same time, Byzantine envoys were pressing King Pedro of Aragon and his wife, Manfred's daughter Constance, to lay claim to the throne of Sicily, assuring them that the island was already on the brink of revolution and eager to receive Pedro and Constance as king and queen. The network of intrigue was carefully spun. Charles of Anjou would never depart on his grand enterprise.

In March 1282, as a crowd of worshippers gathered for vespers outside the cathedral of Palermo, one of Charles' French soldiers tried to molest a Sicilian girl. The bystanders immediately became a mob, as native Sicilians pounced upon the French soldiers of their king in fierce assertion of their rebellion. Within days, the revolt that started with the "Sicilian vespers" had become islandwide. Within months, Pedro of Aragon arrived with Spanish forces to wrest the crown from Charles of Anjou. "In fact," wrote Michael, "if I dare to say that God prepared their [the Sicilians'] liberty and that He did it by my own hands, I would be telling only the truth."[13]

Byzantium was safe; and Michael Palaiologos without the cost of a single Byzantine life had scored the greatest triumph of his reign.

He did not live to enjoy it for long. Now in his late fifties, he was grievously afflicted by an intestinal disorder, though in spite of his ill health, he continued in active leadership of his military forces. Now that Charles of Anjou had been dealt the knock-out blow, he hoped to concentrate his attentions on the Turks. Then news reached him of a rebellion in Thessaly that demanded priority attention. With this goal in mind, he planned to return from his winter palace across the straits to the environs of Constantinople where he would rendezvous with mercenaries supplied by his Tartar son-in-law, Nogai.

Michael's wife Theodora, we are told, warned him against crossing the Sea of Marmara in the foul December weather, but ill as he was, he was determined to undertake the journey. During the crossing he became considerably worse. The imperial party debarked near Pachomios, and soon thereafter, in this obscure Thracian village, Michael died.[14] The usual amenities that surrounded the deathbed of an Orthodox emperor were all lacking, though whether through Michael's own stubborn preference or through the refusal of any Orthodox clergy to attend him is not completely clear. In any case, his son Andronikos was with him when he died; the young man, fearful of popular reaction, ordered his father's body hastily buried in a shallow grave in the dark of the night. Not until several years later were the emperor's remains exhumed, still in surprisingly good condition: he was, people said, too wicked to return to earth.[15] On his son's order Michael's body was conveyed to the city of Selymbria and there quietly interred at an obscure monastery.

Unmourned and unloved, the first of the Palaiologan emperors was gone from the world scene. With the pressure of the Orthodox Church behind her, even his widow Empress Theodora denounced him publicly: she would not hope or pray for his salvation, as it was obviously impossible. It was a sentiment on which the vast majority of Byzantines probably agreed.

In many ways, Michael is the most difficult to understand of all the Palaiologoi. In his determination to preserve his country's independence, Michael might well have been called a Byzantine patriot, had not his willingness to compromise on religious issues, the very matter his subjects held most sacred, won him their undying hatred. Moreover, even in the harsh milieu of his own time, his treatment of little John Laskaris stands out as an act of gross inhumanity. Nevertheless, Michael was undeniably an astute and clever politician. Through more than twenty years of constant struggle, he had managed to hold his empire together against odds that would have overwhelmed a man of lesser ability.

As long as the empire survived, the double eagle that Michael chose as his device continued to fly on Byzantium's banners. Most likely he had "borrowed" the symbol from his predecessor Theodore, who seems to have invented it to signify the fact that the Byzantine state looked both toward Asia and toward Europe;[16] but in time it came to be regarded as the Palaiologan imperial sign, and was enthusiastically imitated by lesser sovereigns as a token of vast prestige. After Michael, the emperors who ruled in Constantinople were, with one exception, his direct descendants. It is not the least of his achievements that Michael was the founder of the dynasty destined to be the longest-lived of any imperial family ever to reign in Byzantium.

4

Trouble in the Land

Perhaps the most striking thing about Michael's son, Andronikos II, was his beard. Orthodox custom decreed that beards be worn, and many Byzantine gentlemen of this period favored a long, flowing masterpiece, sometimes reaching as far as midchest. But the Emperor Andronikos' thick brown beard was a creation uniquely his: cut straight across, it resembled nothing so much as a shovel. He must have been completely satisfied with this effect, for many years later, when his beard had turned snowy white, he was still wearing it in this same fashion.[1]

In many ways, Andronikos II was a better man than his father Michael, but he was also a far less successful emperor. His very lack of those relentless qualities by which Michael had gained his ends proved a grievous failing. In his early twenties when his father died, Andronikos wore the Byzantine crown for forty-six years. He was not neglectful of his duties; on the contrary, he was a conscientious, dedicated sovereign. Intensely Orthodox in his religious policies, he commenced his reign with a denunciation of the Union of Lyons, and he would never pursue to any significant extent his father's leanings toward agreement with the papacy. On the other hand he

29

was always extremely interested in Orthodox theology, so much so that it was often remarked (prophetically, as it turned out) that he would have made an excellent monk. Intelligent, cultured, a patron of learning and the arts, Andronikos seemed to possess many qualifications for leadership. Yet his policies and the advice of those around him often were doomed to failure. His name, Andronikos, which means "man of victory," proved singularly inappropriate, as one defeat followed hard upon another throughout his long reign and most of Asia Minor was irretrievably lost to the Turks.

Andronikos himself was not, and never could be, a soldier like his father Michael. Only once did he take part personally in a military campaign, and that before Michael's death. Dispatched to southern Asia Minor to fight the Turks, Andronikos arrived at the ruined city of Tralleis where his imagination was captivated by the idea of rebuilding this ancient town. Omens found at the site seemed to encourage this plan. He would bestow upon the new city the name of Andronikopolis—or perhaps Palaiologopolis would do just as well. The young man was completely caught up in the project; thousands of settlers were brought in to colonize, and the rebuilt city appeared a thorough success. Four years later, besieged by the Turks who cut off the water supply, Andronikopolis fell.[2] This incident in a small sense reflects the sort of misfortune that plagued Andronikos II all his life: high hopes followed by devastating failure in practically everything he undertook.

Was there some fatal flaw in Andronikos' methods of government that led to such unhappy results, or was it simply inherent in the nature of the times that decay was inevitable? Perhaps the latter is a fairer judgment, for though it is easy to catalogue the problems of the time, it is often hard indeed to formulate what might have been done differently with happier results. The Byzantine Empire by the late thirteenth century was already a nation grown old, a second-rate power unable to compete effectively against the younger, more vigorous states like the Italian republics of Venice and Genoa, the Slavic kingdoms of the Balkan peninsula, or the marauding Turks of Asia Minor, much less against all these rivals at once. Byzantium would never be able to regain the position of commercial leadership in the Eastern Mediterranean that had fallen into the hands of the Genoese and the Venetians, and lacking a healthy economy, the empire could not recover military greatness. There was wealth in abundance among the Byzantine landed nobility but their vast privileges of tax exemption meant that most of this potential revenue was beyond the reach of the imperial treasury. Andronikos II and the emperors who came after him were caught in the hopeless situation of ruling a land in desperate need of changes that could not possibly be carried out.

One great mistake, however, clearly attributable to the Emperor Andronikos himself, was the vast military cutback at the outset of his reign. In order, he said, to save money, the army was reduced in size to only a few thousand troops, and these were practically all hired mercenaries rather than native Byzantines. As for the navy, it was abolished.[3] The empire whose fleet in earlier centuries had ruled the Mediterranean would now depend upon its allies, the Genoese, for naval support.

Andronikos seemed particularly confident of Genoa's friendship for Byzantium. The adventurers and merchants of Genoa who clustered across the Golden Horn in Pera were obviously there to feather their own nests, but Andronikos was so little able to alter the situation that he had to reconfirm their right to maintain the fortifications of Pera. The prosperous little city stood there defiantly, a foreign outpost next door to the imperial capital. The profits of vast foreign trade flowed into Genoese rather than Byzantine hands.

Then, too, there were the Venetians, who in the midst of a war with Genoa, happily moved in and seized for themselves several of the Aegean islands, hitherto Byzantine property. After all, the emperor was an open ally of the Genoese and this made him a mortal foe of Venice. Andronikos finally realized all too clearly the folly of his military cutback, as pieces of his empire were chipped away by the rival Italian republics. Desperately he attempted to rebuild the defense mechanism he had so rashly destroyed. Eventually Byzantium would assemble a new fleet of twenty ships and a new cavalry force of some three thousand men.[4]

In the Balkan area, the rising kingdom of the Serbs loomed as another dangerous and all-too-powerful neighbor. When the emperor tested his new military strength against King Stephen Urosh Milutin of Serbia, the results were not happy for Byzantium.

But perhaps most distressing of all enemies were the Turks of Asia Minor. Pushed westward by the Mongols of Central Asia, vast new hordes of Turkish nomads, including the ancestors of those whom history knows as the Ottomans, swept into Asia Minor during Andronikos' reign. The prosperous territories that John Doukas Vatatzes had welded together with such loving concern, the areas that had for centuries been the real heartland of the Byzantine nation, were almost completely lost in the days of Andronikos II, never again to be regained.

To cope with the worsening situation, in 1303 Andronikos engaged the services of Roger de Flor, commander of a troop of about 6,500 Spanish soldiers of fortune.[5] They called themselves the Catalan Grand Company. Roger himself was not Spanish but German; his name, before translation, was Blum. He had once belonged to—and been expelled from—the Knights Templars; and in his varied career had fought for sundry employers in the Holy Land and Sicily.

Though the King of Sicily was only too glad to be rid of Roger and his followers, to the Byzantine court the arrival of the Catalans seemed at the outset an arrangement that would be mutually profitable in every way. By prior agreement, Roger de Flor was rewarded with the title of Grand Duke. A huge turban-shaped hat trimmed with gold braid and pearls was the symbol of his new dignity. A few days after the Catalans' arrival, Grand Duke Roger was married to Andronikos' sixteen-year-old niece, Princess Maria.

On the wedding night the inhabitants of Constantinople got their first taste of Catalan lawlessness. A brawl broke out between certain Catalans and some Genoese of Pera; and soon people of both parties were rioting in the streets, with the Catalans getting a great advantage over their adversaries. Andronikos sent one of his top aides to investigate, but the infuriated mob tore him to pieces. Order was restored only after the emperor himself appeared at the door of the bridal chamber and pleaded with Roger to command his men to desist in their slaughter of the Genoese. Roger agreed readily enough, and the Catalans obeyed him without question, but not before about three thousand Genoese had been slain.[6]

Andronikos and his advisors vastly preferred that such fighting energy should be directed against the Turks, who in the past few years had practically wiped out the last vestiges of Byzantine rule in Asia Minor. Consequently the Catalan Company was dispatched across the straits, and not long afterward they reported one rousing victory over the enemy. Then more disturbing news began to reach the imperial capital. When they were not fighting Turks, the Catalans, often as not, were ravaging the Christian villages, extorting monies from the Byzantine officials still left in the area, and killing indiscriminately. Orders from Constantinople were completely ignored. It was plain to Andronikos and his son, the Co-emperor Michael IX, that these supposed allies, the Catalans, were a worse foe than the Turks.

Eventually, Roger and some of the other Catalan officers returned to Constantinople to demand payment for their "services." Andronikos tried to placate them with promotions for their leaders. Roger was accorded the rank of Caesar and a costume similar to the emperor's state robe: it differed only in being blue instead of purple. Meanwhile Berenguer Estenza, a Catalan nobleman, received Roger's former title of Grand Duke. The Catalans' reputation of boldness and their utter contempt for established authority are fully demonstrated by Estenza's reaction to his promotion. After repeated acts of rudeness to the emperor, Estenza fearlessly sailed his ship past the sea wall of Blachernai Palace, and in plain sight of many spectators dumped overboard the Grand Ducal bonnet and other regalia he had received from Andronikos.[7]

The emperor, his pride deeply hurt, could of course do nothing. The Catalan leaders had their fierce fighting men behind them. There was no option for Andronikos but to continue his efforts to placate these "allies" with promises of additional pay and other rewards, provided they would return to Asia Minor and reopen their offensive against the Turks. This Roger agreed to do. Then for some unexplained reason, Roger and his associates journeyed from Constantinople to Adrianople, to the palace of the Co-emperor Michael IX. As co-monarch with Andronikos, Michael in theory possessed as much imperial authority as his father, and perhaps the Catalans hoped to extort from him additional funds. It was a grave miscalculation. The young co-emperor—or some advisor in his service—did not hesitate to take the most direct method of solving the problem of Roger de Flor. As the Catalan dignitaries dined in Michael's palace, Roger was seized by the co-emperor's bodyguards and slain, along with a number of his companions.

"What a pity!" exclaimed Michael IX in mock distress when the news was carried upstairs to him.[8]

No Byzantine could actually feel sorry for the removal of the terrible "allies." Deplorable as the method employed might have been, the struggle against the Catalans had reached the point where anything seemed fair. Nevertheless, as Andronikos and Michael quickly realized, though Roger and a few of the other officers were dead, the problem of the Catalan Grand Company was still unsolved. Under new leadership, the unruly soldiers of fortune continued on the rampage in Asia Minor and Thrace for several years longer. They even hired Turkish mercenaries to assist them in their attacks on Byzantine strongholds.

Then, at last, they turned their attention from Thrace to Athens. This ancient city was in the early fourteenth century a quiet provincial outpost. Though the majority of its people were, of course, Greek, Athens was not under the rule of the Byzantine basileus; its duke rather was a Westerner, a descendant of the Frankish crusaders of 1204. The Catalan Company seized Athens in 1311, and for more than seventy years thereafter, the unlikely reality of Spanish rule persisted in the heart of Greece.[9] They never made themselves popular; and for centuries to come when one Greek wished to curse another, he would often exclaim, "May the Catalan vengeance strike you down!" For a while Andronikos and his son Michael continued to be involved in international intrigues to oust the Catalans from Greek soil altogether; yet in the long run such efforts were in vain, and neither lived to see the collapse of the Catalan Duchy of Athens. They could at least take consolation, however, in the fact that the dangerous "allies" had departed from Byzantine territory for good.

5

Trouble at Home

If the land over which Andronikos II reigned was torn by many troubles, so too in time was the emperor's own family. His first wife, the Hungarian princess Anna, had died young, leaving him with two little sons, including the heir to the throne, Michael IX. Andronikos, himself in his early twenties at that time, was determined to remarry. He selected—sight unseen—an Italian princess, Yolande of Montferrat. While Yolande was a granddaughter of the King of Castile, her most outstanding asset in Byzantine eyes was her descent from Boniface of Montferrat, a crusader of 1204 who had become King of Thessaloniki, the "Second City" of the medieval Greek world. Though Thessaloniki was safely back in Byzantine hands by Andronikos' time, he hoped that marriage to Yolande, the current Latin claimant to the throne, would put an end once and for all to Western attempts against this great stronghold. Eleven-year-old Yolande sailed to Constantinople, was baptized into the Orthodox faith as "Irene," and married to the emperor.[1]

As Yolande grew into her teens, she completely won the heart of the basileus. To all outward appearances, it was one of the happiest royal marriages. In due time, three sons were born to Andronikos and Yolande as well as several daughters, though the girl children born before 1294 all died in infancy.

As the father of several sons, the emperor was convinced that he wanted a daughter more than anything on earth. In 1294, when Yolande once again lay awaiting the arrival of an infant, Andronikos prevailed upon the forces of heaven to send him a little girl. He placed a candle before each of twelve icons of the twelve apostles, beseeching them to pray for him and promising (somewhat rashly in view of the possibilities) that he would name his child for the apostle whose candle burned the longest.

When Yolande gave birth to a healthy little daughter, Andronikos was true to his word. Because St. Simon's candle had outlasted all the others, the little princess, he insisted, would be christened Simonis.[2] It was an unheard-of name for a princess, but the emperor's wish was carried out. Among the countless Marias, Theodoras, Helenas, and Irenes of the Palaiologan womenfolk, there is only one Simonis, a girl destined to a most unusual—and unfortunate—life.

Like most nobly born girls, Simonis Palaiologina was fated for a political marriage. Few imperial children in all of Byzantine history, however, were married so young and none suffered more mistreatment at the hands of her spouse than little Simonis, who was only six years old when her parents sent her to marry King Milutin of Serbia. Milutin, whose name meant "Child of Grace," seemed anything but gracious in Byzantine eyes. As the empire's recent foe, he had already seized a large part of Macedonia and was now willing to talk peace only on the condition that he be rewarded with an imperial bride. Milutin was a terrifying monarch in his midforties, who had had three wives already, disposed of all three by various unsavory means, and was now in the market for a genuine Byzantine princess to enhance his prestige; otherwise he and his army would advance on Thessaloniki. Andronikos and

Yolande, and little Simonis, were caught in a most unpleasant situation.

A generation before, Andronikos must have remembered, his own parents Michael VIII and Theodora had considered sending one of their daughters to marry a Serbian prince. At that time, the Empress Theodora had insisted that the Byzantine envoys bring her a full and confidential report on life at the Serbian court. Their findings were most revealing. The Serbian nobility had the table manners of a troop of sheep-thieves, they noted. The king's daughter-in-law wore an "inexpensive" dress and worked at her own spindle. The palace was not even built of stone; it was simply a large wooden building, more like a fortress than a palatial residence. According to the strong-willed Theodora Palaiologina, no Byzantine princess should be subjected to such a barbaric environment, and the prospective alliance had not materialized.[3]

Though the Serbs apparently had not improved at all in the past generation, Andronikos did not have the option that his parents had had of refusing their offers.

In desperation, hoping to avoid sending Simonis to the frightful barbarian Milutin, Andronikos suggested that his widowed sister, Eudokia, would be a more suitable candidate; she, at least, was closer to Milutin's age. But Eudokia, forewarned of the Serbian monarch's character, staunchly refused to be his bride.

There was no alternative but to send Simonis in her place; and the marriage rites were duly celebrated. Still everyone assumed that Milutin would have the decency and common sense to wait till his little bride grew up before expecting her to fulfill her wifely duties.

Unfortunately, Milutin did not wait.[4] Simonis Palaiologina, her young body abused and her hopes of bearing children of her own permanently destroyed, grew up despising the crude barbarian who shared her bed. Yet for all her disdain of him, Milutin seemed genuinely devoted to her in his own fashion. There still remain in

Yugoslavia several frescoes of the sad-eyed child-queen "La Simonida" (as they called her) side by side with her formidable and aging spouse. She grew into an unusually beautiful young woman, who dreamed only of going home to Constantinople, a home she could scarcely remember, and to the father she adored, who had given her her strange, pretty name and who would surely help her, his only daughter, if he knew of her plight.

As years went by, Milutin occasionally allowed Simonis to return to the Byzantine Empire for short visits with her parents. On one such journey, the young Queen of Serbia announced that she simply would not go back to her husband. Informed of this decision, Milutin issued an ultimatum: either Simonis would return or Serbia would declare war on Byzantium. However much he may have wished to help his little daughter, Andronikos was all too well aware of Milutin's superior military strength.

Simonis was promptly sent on the road back to Serbia accompanied by Milutin's ambassadors. Still dreading to see her husband, the young woman made one final attempt to gain her freedom. Before they reached the Serbian border, she dressed herself in a nun's habit. She had taken religious vows, she proclaimed; certainly no one would expect her to return to Milutin now.

The Serbian ambassadors were temporarily baffled. Not so Simonis' half-brother, Prince Constantine, who happened to be in the area. When he learned what she had done, Constantine demanded that she give up such foolery, as he roughly tore the nun's robe in which she had hoped to find her escape. In tears, Simonis was handed back to Milutin's envoys.[5]

It was not until she was twenty-three that Milutin died, and subsequently she returned to her father's court for good.

During the years that Simonis languished in the palace of the Serbian king, back in Constantinople the growing arguments of Yolande and Andronikos were the liveliest subject of court gossip. Yolande was satisfied that Simonis was well provided for as Queen of Serbia; indeed she seems to have considered Milutin a perfectly satisfactory son-in-law, and it was her habit to send him annually a bejeweled cap that looked much like the emperor's crown. Yes, Yolande thought, Simonis' future was secure. But what was to be the inheritance of Yolande and Andronikos' three sons: John, Theodore, and Demetrios?

Yolande despised her stepsons, especially young Michael IX, whom Andronikos recognized as co-emperor. Why should the dead Anna's son have a crown and her boys nothing? The subject was becoming Yolande's sole preoccupation. The solution was so simple if only Andronikos could be made to see it: he would have to divide his empire as if it were a private estate and give some part of it to each of his sons.

To this suggestion, Andronikos Palaiologos resolutely answered no. This sort of thing simply was not done. He would not deprive Michael of his full inheritance. Yolande pleaded, coaxed, pouted, stormed, even threatened suicide, but Andronikos would not give in.[6] And after all their years together, Yolande decided she no longer loved Andronikos at all.

Finally in 1303 or 1304, when they had been married for more than twenty years, she left him.[7] She was after all Queen of Thessaloniki in her own right, or so she claimed, and henceforth she would reside in her own city. Andronikos, weary of her incessant nagging, cannot have been too sorry to see her go. Her departure, nonetheless, cast a cloud of shame over the emperor. He could not divorce her; in the Orthodox world only death or entry into the monastic life dissolved the marriage bond, and Yolande had no intention of becoming a nun. The basileus and basilissa would simply and permanently remain apart, he in Constantinople and she in Thessaloniki, where she delighted in entertaining her guests with malicious, all-too-personal details of her life with Andronikos.

Her ambitious intrigues for her children never

faltered. To John, the eldest, Andronikos finally assigned governorship of Thessaloniki, an arrangement that seemingly satisfied Yolande. The young man died a few years later. For her second son, Theodore, Yolande achieved considerably more success. On the death of her brother, the Marquis of Montferrat, the right to his lands in Italy fell to her. The empress duly transferred her claim to Theodore, who departed for his new principality. There within a short time, the Byzantine prince would become thoroughly Italianized. Probably he had learned the language from his mother in his childhood; now he discarded his stiff brocaded robes for the more comfortable garb of thirteenth-century Italy, and sacrilegious as it seemed from the Orthodox viewpoint, he shaved off his beard! In later years when *Teodoro Paleologo* returned to the Byzantine Empire on occasional visits, his family scarcely recognized him.[8]

For her youngest son, Demetrios, Yolande could think of nothing better than to have him "adopted" as a son by his own sister, the childless Queen Simonis of Serbia, and her husband Milutin. This plan failed miserably, as Demetrios was most unhappy among the Serbs and preferred the comforts of his father's court in Constantinople.

Yolande herself lived on in Thessaloniki until 1317, estranged forever from her imperial husband. Then, when she died, it was discovered that she had willed her substantial fortune not to her children after all, but to Andronikos. The old emperor designated half of this bequest for badly needed repairs on the ancient church of Hagia Sophia; the remainder he divided among the surviving children that Yolande had borne him: Theodore, Demetrios, and Simonis. For himself, he kept nothing at all.[9]

6

Imperial Cousins

Though Andronikos' difficulties with Yolande over
the years had proved a grave cause of dissension in the
imperial household, the emperor could take comfort in the
loyalty of his eldest son and co-emperor, Michael. The
young man was a gallant if none-too-successful military
leader, and Andronikos, who would never fight at all,
entrusted him with leadership of the Byzantine army as
well as a larger share in the business of government
administration than practically any co-emperor before
him. The Palaiologos dynasty seemed well on the way to
becoming a permanent institution: Michael VIII, Andronikos II, Michael IX, and then in 1297[1] Michael and his wife
Xene of Armenia had their first son, unquestioned heir to
the throne of his fathers. In accordance with the usual
custom of the imperial family, they named him Andronikos for his grandfather the emperor. It was about this time
that people began to forget that Andronikos II had ever
been a young man; though he was only thirty-eight, an
uncommonly young grandfather, he was irrevocably "Old
Andronikos" to his subjects.

Apparently the proud grandfather did not mind, for
the little grandson who shared his name was the apple of
his eye, a bright spot in his otherwise rather unhappy

existence. The small prince was spoiled and petted by a host of adoring relatives. He grew up good-natured but irresponsible, as capricious as the wind and just as unrestrainable.

It was about a year or two before young Andronikos was born that another child who was destined to play an extremely important role in his life was born into the imperial family. John Angelos Palaiologos Kantakouzenos was only a distant cousin of the throne-heir, but his ambitious mother, Theodora, was careful to insert the "Palaiologos" in his name to emphasize the fact that kinship did exist between her John and the emperors. John was the center of his mother's world; even as he lay in his cradle, Theodora Kantakouzene knew he would be her only child. Her husband, the provincial governor of the Peloponnese, had died some weeks or months before the infant's birth,[2] and she had vowed herself then and there to a life of celibacy. Henceforth, though she was young, aristocratic, and immeasurably wealthy, she would devote herself only to the ideals of pious widowhood so idealized by Byzantine society and to the upbringing of her fatherless son. John, she was determined, would take his place among the princes of the Great Palace, and though we know next to nothing of the details, in time the boy came to live with the imperial household.

Though they were only distant cousins, the crown prince Andronikos and John Kantakouzenos grew up to be closer than most brothers. Years later, when Andronikos was long dead, Kantakouzenos recalled of his friend: "Such was the union of our two souls that it surpassed even the friendship of Orestes and Pylades."[3] Yet in many ways it was an unlikely friendship. As the imperial cousins grew to manhood, it was obvious to all who knew them that Kantakouzenos was the thinker, clear-headed and competent, while Andronikos was the happy-go-lucky sort who took life as it came, who vastly preferred an evening of carousing about town or enjoying the favors of his latest mistress to one spent in serious political discussion.

Though they looked nothing at all alike, the two young men must have been almost exactly the same size, for they could—and did—wear each other's clothes and even shoes. Andronikos delighted in seeing Kantakouzenos in the costumes designed for the crown prince of Byzantium.

While his habits of sharing his wardrobe with his friend perhaps seemed just another sign of Andronikos' immaturity, there were other, more disturbing indications of his failure to take seriously his role as heir to the throne of Byzantium. Young Andronikos was still in his teens when he discovered the magic of buying on credit; all it took was a promissory note signed with that marvelous name that was his grandfather's as well as his own: Andronikos Palaiologos. What the young man could not pay, his grandfather the emperor always paid for him. Who could wish for a more pleasant arrangement? The prince cheerfully squandered funds he did not possess, spent his days hunting and horse racing and his nights carousing.[4] Women found the charming young man practically irresistible, and his romantic conquests were a perennial subject of gossip.

It was his unwise involvement with a certain woman that led him to unsuspected tragedy.[5]

Andronikos was about twenty-three when he became deeply infatuated with a new mistress, a lady of aristocratic birth. He never dreamed of marrying the woman (for after all, imperial marriages were made for politics, not for love, and he was already saddled with a little German wife, Adelheid-Irene of Brunswick). It was his mistress, nonetheless, who was the object of his deepest devotion. Almost every night he could be found at her home; he was perfectly happy, it seemed, and then an ugly seed of jealousy began to ripen in his mind. His lady loved another; he was sure of it. Very well, then, he would trap his rival. Andronikos stationed men to lurk in a dark passage near his mistress' door. If any man is seen approaching the place, pounce upon him, he admonished them.

Andronikos' younger brother, Prince Manuel, knew nothing of this plot, but he did know where he was most likely to find Andronikos, and having some news of urgent importance to convey to him, Manuel sought out the home of the mistress. There in the pitch darkness of the narrow street, the hired thugs stood waiting for the man who dared to interfere with their master's woman. Without warning, they fell upon Manuel. It was only later that they realized the identity of the body that lay at their feet, beaten to death.

Though he had not struck the blows with his own hands, Andronikos Palaiologos had killed his brother. Though it was an accident, though he might weep copious tears and protest his innocence to the world, Andronikos was a fratricide. The news was carried quickly to the co-emperor Michael IX in Adrianople[6] and Michael, who loved both his sons, found the pain too deep to bear. He was in poor health in any event; he apparently already had a severe heart condition, but it was the news of Manuel's murder that led to his fatal heart attack.

For the old Emperor Andronikos II, this double tragedy was the end of a lifetime's plans. Michael was dead—his serious, hard-working son, the heir whose rights he had defended even though it had cost him the love of the fiery Yolande and made him the laughingstock of his people. And in place of Michael, the immediate heir to the throne was now young Andronikos, impulsive, careless, and worst of all, the real cause of Michael and Manuel's deaths.

Old Andronikos had always been deeply devoted to the grandson who bore his name; he had forgiven a thousand small transgressions on the basis of his youth and high-spiritedness. Murder he could not forgive. The young man had sinned the sin of Cain, and like Cain, he must become an outcast.

7

The Disinherited

It is not easy to disinherit the heir to the throne, Andronikos II would discover. Young Andronikos had his faults, but he also had his friends. Pleasant-tempered, likable, never one to insist on great formality, an excellent horseman and hunter, young Andronikos naturally attracted a following of young Byzantine nobles who encouraged him to demand his rights. Most of all, there was his friend and cousin, John Kantakouzenos, that brilliant, intense young man with almond eyes and strangely Oriental features, who was unquestionably ready to lay down his life for young Andronikos. More important, Kantakouzenos was prepared to be extremely generous with his money, or rather with his mother's money. Theodora Kantakouzene, it was widely known, possessed sufficient funds to finance a small revolution or two singlehandedly.[1]

The old emperor moved as cautiously as the intensity of his despair would permit him. There had to be a substitute heir to the throne, someone who would be absolutely loyal, who would never hurt him as young Andronikos had. It is little wonder that the old emperor began to think seriously of naming as his heir the one person in the world who he believed loved him unselfishly: Michael Katharos, the illegitimate child of the emperor's own son, Prince Constantine.[2] Neither of Michael's own parents had wanted him, but a child with the precious Palaiologos blood in his veins could scarcely grow up unprovided for. Michael was just a boy when old Andronikos took him into the imperial palace. There he was reared as befitted a prince; when he was grown, it was felt, he might prove a useful bridegroom for some barbarian princess with whose people Byzantium sought alliance.

As it turned out, little Michael adored his grandfather, the emperor. Old Andronikos must have often thought how this young man, handsome, bright, and mild-mannered, seemed far better qualified for future rulership than the legitimate heir. More and more often, Michael Katharos appeared at his grandfather's side on public occasions. Then old Andronikos drew up a revised oath of allegiance which his nobles were to be required to take: to Andronikos himself and *whomever* he might designate as his heir.[3]

On the other hand, it was too dangerous to banish young Andronikos outright; best to keep him in Constantinople where he could be watched closely. Grandfather and grandson continued to live in the same palace, the younger Andronikos knowing full well the hatred that the elder did not even try to conceal. For four months, the emperor refused to speak a single word to him; when other court dignitaries were granted permission to sit in the emperor's presence, old Andronikos forced his grandson to remain standing. The air at the Byzantine court was charged with the high tension of inevitable conflict to come.

The young men of influence felt inevitably drawn to the side of the dynamic, chivalrous, affable young Andronikos. The old emperor, they reasoned, was simply too old. He spent altogether too much time in philosophical discussions with the other old men of his generation. He and his friend Theodore Metochites were perennially engrossed in astrology, seemingly useless studies of the calendar, and attempts to probe into the future.[4] Yet the future belonged to the young, to the prince whose military abilities already far surpassed those of his grandfather. Old Andronikos did not know how to fight; under young Andronikos, things could be different for Byzantium. The powerful supporters of the young prince urged rebellion, stating that he must depose his grandfather and seize the crown for himself alone.

In light of these developments, old Andronikos could scarcely have taken a more unwise step than the one he finally took. After four months of glowering at his grandson, he had young Andronikos formally charged with treason. The trial was to be held in the palace. The old emperor convoked the nobles whom he felt he could rely upon, and the patriarch, and before this august assembly sat young Andronikos in the "seat of the accused."

No one anticipated what the prince intended to do. Scarcely had his grandfather begun his tirade, when young Andronikos interrupted him. In moving terms, the grandson confessed that he had proved unworthy in small things, that he had given too much of his time to frivolous pleasures, but, he added, his loyalty to his grandfather was absolute.

This was more than the old man could bear. Casting imperial dignity to the winds, oblivious to what those around him might think, Andronikos II screamed at his grandson. The young man was not even a Christian, he stormed.

Andronikos the Younger answered calmly, in words that his friend John Kantakouzenos recalled long after: "If you have made up your mind to condemn me without hearing, do with me what you like, and at once. If not, judge me according to the law!" The prince was unquestionably a brave man; but he also knew, as his grandfather did not, that some of his powerful friends and their men at arms were lurking even at that moment within the palace.

Kantakouzenos and the others would see to it that no real harm befell him.[5]

The strategic moment had come; a courier from these supporters of the young Andronikos entered the room with a message for the emperor: if any injustice is done, there will be war. Confused and humiliated, old Andronikos muttered something about an immediate reconciliation, and young Andronikos agreed to take a new oath of loyalty to his grandfather. For the time being, the situation was saved, but no one, least of all the two Andronikoi, believed that the deep hurts they had both suffered could be healed so easily.

Not many weeks later, Andronikos the Younger went to Adrianople, claiming that he was going hunting though actually he went to muster an army.[6] He was insisting now that his grandfather reconfirm him as co-emperor. To attract volunteers, he offered lavish and unrealistic favors. The old emperor's high taxes had always been unpopular; young Andronikos promised that when *he* became emperor there would be a vast tax reduction—indeed, for some really loyal supporters, complete exemption.[7]

The years 1321 and 1322 witnessed considerable fighting as well as more than one attempt at compromise. Young Andronikos, usually with Kantakouzenos at his side, led his troops in person. Far more able as a soldier than as a financier, the prince possessed genuine military ability, and as for money, who needed to worry? Theodora Kantakouzene's strongboxes would always be open for such a good cause.

At one point the emperor agreed to recognize his grandson as co-emperor and a truce was effected actually dividing the lands of the empire between them. But no coronation was held for young Andronikos and it was not long before hostilities broke out again. Finally in February 1325, after a seemingly lasting truce had been in effect for some months, young Andronikos achieved what he wanted: with all the sacred rites of the ancient ceremony, his grandfather crowned him co-emperor, Andronikos III.[8] Only one disturbing incident marred the joyful occasion: as old Andronikos was riding to Hagia Sophia, his horse tripped and fell in a mud puddle.[9] The superstitious emperor as well as many of the spectators considered this an unmistakably evil omen.

Nevertheless, for the present, all seemed well. Peace was restored to the land and to the imperial family, if only the two Andronikoi could continue to work together in harmony.

8

The Bride from Savoy

For Andronikos the Younger, one of the first important pieces of state business to be dealt with after his coronation was the search for a suitable bride. His German wife Adelheid had given him only one son who had died in infancy, and now Adelheid herself was dead. For a long time, court gossips had whispered of young Andronikos' affection for Queen Simonis, Milutin's widow. It is difficult to know how much truth underlies these rumors. Though she was not much older than he, Simonis was young Andronikos' half-aunt; and even had they wished to marry, Orthodoxy strictly forbade such a match as incestuous.

Though apparently he had never cared much for Adelheid, Andronikos still seemed to think that selection of a wife from Western Europe was a wise policy. Count Edouard of Savoy in the Italian Swiss Alps had a little sister, Johanna, a pretty, blonde princess in her teens.[1] On first glance it is hard to imagine what Andronikos hoped to gain politically by alliance with the distant land of Savoy. But then he, the co-emperor of the war-torn state of Byzantium, was no prize on the European marriage market. Perhaps the Savoyard princess was the best he could hope for.[2]

The negotiations were duly carried out, and after a leisurely journey of five months, Johanna reached Constantinople with a ship full of Savoyard nobles and ladies. A Roman Catholic, she now joined the Orthodox Church, and in good Orthodox tradition changed her name to Anne. Eight months later (for the bride-to-be became ill and the wedding had to be postponed), Andronikos and Anne were married, and to all outward appearances, happily so. Andronikos liked the Savoyards, and some of them stayed to become a permanent part of the imperial entourage. There were tournaments with all the trimmings of Western chivalry; Andronikos took part in person and thoroughly enjoyed playing at knighthood. His deeds of valor were widely acclaimed; he was, it was commonly said, as skilled as the celebrated knights of Burgundy. Kantakouzenos apparently did not share his friend's enthusiasm for this dangerous sport, and probably with a bit of jealousy toward Andronikos' new friendships, asserted that such happenings had never been seen in Byzantium before.[3]

Traditionalists of the older generation were more disapproving. They professed shock that the young co-emperor exposed himself to such needless risks. They were critical, too, of his informality. He did not even insist that persons entering his presence wear the standard turbanlike headgear prescribed by etiquette, and many of his Savoyard friends were seen in "Latin hats."[4] Such disrespect for tradition was a sure sign of the end of the world—or at least of the empire—grumbled the prominent historian of the court, Nikephoros Gregoras.[5] Andronikos III ignored such criticism. The excessive ceremonialism of the Byzantine court had always irritated him, and his new-found Western friends would discover him to be easily approachable, affable, and unaffected.

Anne of Savoy, for her part, had to learn to endure John Kantakouzenos.

Kantakouzenos was never far away. When Andronikos and Anne went on their honeymoon, he was among the crowd of nobles who accompanied them. This was an occasion he would long remember, for on the journey, he was waylaid by a band of Turks who killed his horse from under him. Kantakouzenos himself escaped unhurt,[6] though in light of later developments, one suspects that Anne would have been glad had the Turks disposed of him once and for all.

The family strife of the Palaiologoi had not really been solved by the coronation of young Andronikos as co-emperor. For a while, it is true, the mutual distrust of grandfather and grandson simmered beneath the surface, but in 1327, the year after the marriage of Andronikos III and Anne, full-scale war broke out again. John Kantakouzenos as grand domestic (commander) of his master's forces entrusted his civil responsibilities in the treasury department to their ally, Alexios Apokavkos, and rode off with young Andronikos to direct military operations in person.

For the Serbs and the Bulgars, the civil war of the Andronikoi was a chance to further their own fortunes at Byzantium's expense. Both sides employed these Slavic mercenaries in their struggle for power. The land was ravaged; as in all wars, the common folk were the real victims. The Byzantine countryside was devastated, non-combatants slain; decent, law-abiding folk who cared not at all which emperor won out so long as there might be peace, were driven from their homes.

The only good thing to be said for this last round in the Wars of the Andronikoi is that it was short. One dark night in May 1328, conspirators in Constantinople who favored the young emperor arranged to open St. Romanos' gate to the forces of Andronikos III.[7]

Andronikos II, after a stormy reign of forty-six years, was compelled to abdicate. He was seventy now and going blind, his long life full of struggles that scarcely seemed worth the effort. Nikephoros Gregoras, who was closely acquainted with the events that occurred that night, records the old emperor's plea for mercy when he came face to face with his victorious grandson. "My son," Andronikos II said, "since God has this day taken the scepter away from me and granted it to you, I ask one grace of you, in return for many I have given you since the day of your birth. . . . Do not shed violently the blood from which you have sprung. . . . Respect these hands which held you many times when you were still a baby. . . . Pity a broken reed, thrown about by fortune, and do not break it a second time. . . . Observe how uncertain and everchanging things are, beginning with my own fate. Observe the end of my long life. Watch with wonder how one night has found me emperor for so many years and left me the subject of another."[8]

Young Andronikos embraced and kissed his grandfather, promised him that he might stay on in the palace, and ordered that all should treat him with respect. As the months passed, however, the old ex-emperor complained that he was receiving no respect at all: even the palace servants were heard to scoff at him. In January 1330, he could bear it no longer, and decided to become a monk. He changed his name to Brother Anthony, but apparently he did not enter a cloister, for two years later, there is a description of him living in a private home with his widowed daughter Queen Simonis to take care of him. There one evening the ex-emperor received a visitor, his old friend the historian, Gregoras. They talked together for many hours, Gregoras scarcely dreaming that old Andronikos—Brother Anthony—would die later that night.

Now there was only one possible claimant to the Byzantine throne: Andronikos III, who at such great cost had fought for his birthright and won. And there was only one power behind that throne: the brilliant, crafty mind of John Palaiologos Kantakouzenos, the imperial cousin.

Manuel Palaiologos and his family
Service de Documentation Photographique, Paris

**row 1 Andronikos III, John VI Kantakouzenos, John V
row 2 Andronikos IV, John VII, Manuel II
row 3 John VIII, Constantine XI, Chlorus**
Fotografia Editrice, Modena

John Kantakouzenos
Bibliothèque Nationale, Paris

Michael Palaiologos
Manuscript miniature. Cod. Monacensis. Gr. 442
Staatsbibliothek, Munich

9

Andronikos III

Soon after he was installed as sole basileus, Andronikos III received a plea for financial aid from the Holy
Roman Emperor, Ludwig IV of Bavaria. Ludwig was hard
pressed indeed to expect help from the impoverished
Byzantines, but of course Andronikos did not want the
German envoys to realize the absurdity of their sovereign's request. He heard them out and then suggested that
they talk with Kantakouzenos, knowing that his friend
would, as always, have a solution to the dilemma.

Kantakouzenos' reply to the Germans took Andronikos by surprise. We cannot send money, he said in
effect, but we will gladly send soldiers to fight on Ludwig's
behalf. Andronikos was momentarily taken aback, for
soldiers were no easier come by than money. Kantakouzenos, who understood the whole situation better than his
master, explained patiently: the Germans probably do not
need troops, and even if they should accept the offer, they
cannot do so without further communications with Ludwig that would take several months. If they refuse, he
reasoned, we are none the worse off; if by some slim
possibility they should accept, we will continue to stall for
time. Eventually the crisis will have blown over, and we
won't have had to contribute anything.[1]

Andronikos was satisfied. His friend John Kantakouzenos was brilliant beyond all doubt. The response to Ludwig's embarrassing request was just one of the many instances in which Kantakouzenos had seemed instinctively to know what to do. What an emperor he would have made!

Then in the summer of 1329, Andronikos was severely wounded in the knee in a battle against the Ottoman Turks at Pelekanon in Bithynia.[2] As Kantakouzenos and Anne hovered by his bedside a few days later, the young emperor spoke worriedly about the future. He had no son; if he were to die, what would keep the empire from plunging again into civil war? There was only one way to save the situation: he would have Kantakouzenos crowned as his co-emperor. It was the greatest gift he could give him, and he was ready to bestow it freely. Even Anne seemed agreeable; she had not yet given her husband a son—she dared not protest.

Strangely enough, Kantakouzenos was not eager to accept.[3] Consecration as emperor, he knew, was an irrevocable act; once the sacred rite had been performed, a man must live and die as emperor or else, like his master's grandfather, end his days in disgrace as a monk. There could be no return to one's former comfortable life as a high-ranking noble. John Kantakouzenos had his own family to think about. His wife, Irene Asen, and their young children might indeed relish promotion to princely status, but should he ultimately fall from power, the whole Kantakouzenos family would most likely fall with him into monastic obscurity. No, it simply would not be practical to accept the crown, he reasoned. Andronikos would recover from his wounds. He would yet have a son to succeed him. The emperor, confronted by his friend's strange stubbornness, had no choice but to shelve his plans for bestowing the co-emperorship upon him.

Then, six months later, in January 1330, Andronikos became ill. Though he was only thirty-two years old, he felt so certain he was dying that he was determined to abdicate and become a monk.[4] With the dramatic intensity that had always characterized his actions, the emperor confided his plans to Kantakouzenos. It would be both wise and pious to die in the odor of sanctity, with all his sins forgiven. . . .

Again, Kantakouzenos protested, horrorstricken at the irrevocability of what the emperor threatened to do. Suppose Andronikos should take the monastic vows and recover? Such a thing had happened before in imperial history; centuries earlier, Isaac Komnenos, believing he was dying of pneumonia, had become a monk and then, recovering his health, had to cope with the fact that he was a monk for life. It was entirely too dangerous, Kantakouzenos declared, and ill as he was, Andronikos understood his friend's logic. He would be a wretched monk, if actually compelled to live the monastic life for any length of time whatsoever. He agreed to wait a little while, to see if he might recover.

In later years, Andronikos would never forget how his friend had saved him from what could have been the most foolish decision of his life. It was another bond between them.

Finally on June 18, 1332, at the castle fortress of Didymoteichos, Anne of Savoy gave birth to the long-awaited male heir.[5] The delighted Andronikos ordered a series of tournaments to celebrate the birth of his son. According to the custom of the centuries, the little boy should have been named Michael for his paternal grandfather; but Andronikos had never cared much for tradition. His eldest son would have the name of the man who had always been his dearest friend: John.

It is not difficult to imagine what Anne thought of this choice. Perhaps she consoled herself by thinking that little John, blond, fair-skinned, so like his mother, was really named for her, for after all she had been called Johanna when she was a girl in Savoy. In any event, the child's name was not so important as the fact that he was born. By his very existence the infant John Palaiologos would have to erase any thought Andronikos still might have of making John Kantakouzenos co-emperor.

In the years that followed, Andronikos III continued his wars against his near neighbors with considerable success. Epiros and Thessaly, Greek-speaking territories that had long resisted the rule of the basileus, were subdued and annexed to the empire.[6] Most of the troops fighting for Byzantium were mercenaries, often including Ottoman Turks who were excellent soldiers. No one, however, seemed to reflect on the irony of these foreigners' plundering of Greek lands in the name of the Greek emperor.

In all these military enterprises, Kantakouzenos played a leading role. On campaign, he was the emperor's constant companion, day and night. Unquestionably, it was Kantakouzenos who masterminded practically all the important decisions that were made. Andronikos granted his friend the privilege of writing his signature in red ink—a right reserved for the emperor—and orders so signed by Kantakouzenos were obeyed as if they came from the basileus himself.

Meanwhile, Theodora Kantakouzene, ever devoted to her son's best interests, endeavored to win the confidence and friendship of Anne of Savoy. Anne, understandably, preferred the companionship of the Italian ladies who had come with her from Savoy.

She bore Andronikos other children: a second son, duly named Michael, another son, Theodore, and three daughters.[7] On the surface, she seemed genuinely devoted to her imperial husband. As for Kantakouzenos, she declared she loved him as much as she loved her own brother, the Count of Savoy.[8] Anne had a distinctive knack for colorful statements that seemed to be in her own best interests.

In June 1341, when Andronikos was attending a
church council in Hagia Sophia, he suddenly became
violently ill. Four days later, he was to die.[9] Tormented by
fears of the future, he insisted as he lay on his deathbed
that Anne and Kantakouzenos join hands and swear their
loyalty to him, to each other, and to the empire. Kantakouzenos, whatever his faults, was basically a man of his
word. He had never wavered in his loyalty to Andronikos,
and there was every reason to hope he would serve the
new Emperor John V just as faithfully. The problematical
factor was Anne, who as an emperor's mother would
possess far greater prestige than she ever enjoyed as an
emperor's wife.

10

The War of Anne
and Kantakouzenos

When Andronikos III died on the fifteenth of June 1341, his son John V was a few days short of nine years old. The prospect of a long regency loomed on the horizon. Even though the dying Andronikos had neglected to designate a regent,[1] it was inevitable that John Kantakouzenos should expect to play a leading role in directing affairs of state for the little boy who bore his name. Just as inevitably, perhaps, Anne of Savoy threw all her energies into an outburst of hatred against this man whom she had heretofore been compelled to treat with cordial respect. Between them, Anne and Kantakouzenos would tear the empire apart; practically all the troubles Byzantium faced in her last century either originated or intensified in the terrible strife of Anne and Kantakouzenos.

Who was to blame? It is easy to dislike Anne—shallow, selfish, spiteful Anne, forever an alien at heart, with no real concern for the Byzantine state. Was she driven to act as she did from a desire to protect her child, one may wonder, and the overwhelming impression is that she was not. It is extremely unlikely, in view of his undoubted devotion to the late Andronikos, that Kantakouzenos would have harmed his little son or sought to deprive him of his crown, and Anne must have realized this. She seems rather to have been most concerned to exercise power, and it was her misfortune that she lacked the ability to do so constructively.

Yet strangely enough, throughout the long struggle between Anne and Kantakouzenos most of the ordinary Byzantine citizens supported Anne and her son rather than the ambitious aristocrat who was her rival. Dynastic loyalty was a large factor here: the common folk trusted the Palaiologoi to treat them more fairly than Kantakouzenos, who was a representative of the noble class.[2]

John Kantakouzenos is himself a difficult figure to evaluate. Like Anne, he wanted power, but unlike her, he possessed a genuine gift for statesmanship. His years as the grand domestic and power behind Andronikos' throne had amply demonstrated his capabilities. He knew if he were to be excluded from Anne's regime, he would see his work undone. It was Kantakouzenos' tragedy that, though he was destined to be one of the empire's destroyers, he almost certainly loved his country and wanted sincerely to guide her to a position of renewed strength.

From his own personal fortune, Kantakouzenos paid the funeral expenses of his friend Andronikos. The grieving widow Anne momentarily expressed her appreciation and trust in him, and in the days immediately following the funeral it seemed that Kantakouzenos had the realm well in hand. On a single day he is reported to have dispatched 500 letters, informing important persons of the changes that were taking place. Anne, who could always be counted on for an inappropriate and graceless remark, commented when she saw Kantakouzenos that he seemed like Andronikos returned to life.[3]

But if on the surface there was seeming harmony between the empress and the grand domestic, Anne's ears were ever open to Kantakouzenos' enemies. As weeks passed, she began to exhibit favor more and more openly for the patriarch John Kalekas and the smooth-talking admiral Alexios Apokavkos, two of his bitterest foes. Apokavkos was a particularly sinister character. Once an ardent supporter of Kantakouzenos, he had now become equally ardent in his alleged determination to uphold the rights of Empress Anne. Secretly he was planning (as was discovered later) to kidnap the young Emperor John and thus attain supreme power for himself.

There could not have been a worse time for such factional intrigues at the Byzantine court, for on the foreign scene, Milutin's grandson Tsar Stephen Dushan, the great soldier monarch of Serbia, was bent upon expanding his state at Byzantium's expense. Before the summer was over, an incursion of Dushan's Serbs on the Macedonian frontier called for Kantakouzenos' departure from the capital at the head of the armed forces. With the grand domestic absent, his enemies prepared to move against him. Rumors were circulated to the effect that the Patriarch Kalekas had offered his blessing to anyone who might rid the world of Kantakouzenos. While this report may well be exaggerated, it is certain that Anne's henchmen plundered Kantakouzenos' city home. All his moveables were carried off by the happy looters, and the bare house itself was rendered unlivable by their acts of wanton destruction. The homes of some of his friends were likewise devastated. Even worse, his mother, Theodora Kantakouzene, and his youngest son Andronikos were placed under house arrest. Not long afterwards, Theodora was incarcerated in a wretched cell.

When news of these atrocities reached him, Kantakouzenos determined to act. A truce has been arranged with Dushan; Kantakouzenos returned to his family stronghold at Didymoteichos and there, in a hastily planned ceremony on October 26, 1341, scarcely four months since Andronikos' death, he had himself officially proclaimed emperor. He was, he declared, the "spiritual brother" of Andronikos, and his claim to the throne was based on this relationship deeper than the ties of blood.[4]

For three days he dressed in the formal purple robes of the basileus; then, with a flair for the dramatic calculated to make a deep impression upon his contemporaries, he appeared in a mourning robe of plain white, and vowed publicly that he would continue to wear mourning for his beloved "brother" until the wrongs that were being done in the name of the little Emperor John were avenged. He had no quarrel with Anne; he placed great emphasis on this point by having her name and that of her young son mentioned before his own in his proclamation of sovereignty. His quarrel was rather with Anne's unscrupulous advisors. If she wanted peace, he would cooperate to the fullest; if she refused, he vowed, he would have himself solemnly anointed and consecrated as emperor, an act far more sacred and binding than this mere proclamation of his claim to the title. Spurred on by her advisors, Anne decided she wanted nothing to do with peace. The patriarch Kalekas did his part by announcing the official excommunication of Kantakouzenos. This was followed in November by the coronation of little John V.

Meanwhile, through the long and dreadfully cold winter of 1341-42, Kantakouzenos remained in Didymoteichos surrounded by a small body of loyal retainers. A man of less determination would have been vastly discouraged, for practically every advantage appeared to be in the hands of his enemies. Kantakouzenos, however, was resolved to continue the struggle, and before long his agents were in contact with the great Tsar Dushan himself. This decision to ally himself with the empire's enemy against what seemed a greater enemy within has earned Kantakouzenos much criticism. Yet he knew that the war that was brewing would have to be fought largely with mercenaries; Byzantium's own armed forces were entirely too meager. From his point of view, alliance with Stephen Dushan was a clever and completely logical move.

When spring came again, after seemingly interminable months of heavy snow and rain, John Kantakouzenos with about two thousand troops departed for the Serbian frontier. His wife, Irene Asen, was left in command of Didymoteichos.

In the next few years, Kantakouzenos experienced widely varied fortunes of war. At one point his personal army dwindled to a mere 500 men. About this same time he received word that his mother, who was well up in her sixties, had died in prison, a victim of the mistreatment she had received there. Adversity seemed only to strengthen Kantakouzenos' determination to fight on. His alliance with Dushan at least seemed mutually profitable, though it would soon become clear to both parties that a pact built on no other foundation than common hatred of the regime in Constantinople could not endure for long. Kantakouzenos sought allies elsewhere, while Dushan engaged in secret intrigues with Anne's henchmen in the capital.

As he so often had done while Andronikos was still alive, Kantakouzenos turned for aid to the Turks. It was with Turkish assistance that he was able to relieve the siege of Didymoteichos, invested by his enemies not long after his departure from that stronghold. Throughout the weeks of siege before this help arrived, his wife Irene had proved a courageous and capable organizer of the city's defenses. It was an achievement she would always remember proudly and about which reputedly she would often reminisce. The sources have little to say of the Empress Irene Asen Kantakouzene. Perhaps she is seen most clearly in her role as the defender of Didymoteichos, her husband's full partner in his struggle for the throne.

As Kantakouzenos' faction appeared to be gaining in strength, Stephen Dushan, whose own purposes were better served by support of the weaker of the warring claimants to the throne, openly switched to a realignment of Serbia with Anne of Savoy. John Kantakouzenos countered by a new alliance with the Ottoman Turkish Sultan Orkhan. In return for military assistance, the imperial claimant offered a prize hitherto undreamed of by a Moslem prince. Kantakouzenos had three young daughters, each as beautiful, said the Turks, as the *houris* of paradise. The second of these, Theodora Kantakouzene, would be sent to grace the sultan's harem.[5]

What may have been the young lady's reaction to this arrangement is difficult to imagine. In any event, she was sent; and in the same year, her father, now in a far more secure position than at any time since the start of the struggle five years earlier, actually had himself consecrated as basileus in Adrianople.[6] The rite was performed by Lazaros, the titular patriarch of Jerusalem, and perhaps was not so completely valid as if it had been done by the patriarch of Constantinople. Nevertheless, from this day on, Kantakouzenos could lawfully appear in imperial garb. For the past five years, he had remained steadfast in his vow to dress only in solid white; but now the time of mourning was over. Constantinople would soon be in his grasp.

Meanwhile in the imperial capital, Anne presided over an increasingly worsening situation with no apparent understanding. Early in the struggle she pawned the crown jewels and plate to the Venetian Republic for 30,000 ducats, a loan she could never repay and that would haunt her son, John V, for years.

The empress' cause received a great setback when Alexios Apokavkos, who had become probably her staunchest supporter, was murdered in the summer of 1345. His end was singularly appropriate; while inspecting the progress in construction of a new prison he had ordered built, he was pounced upon and slain by a band of forced laborers—political prisoners whom he had incarcerated there. Then Anne's other henchman, the Patriarch Kalekas, incurred her wrath for obscure reasons clear only to the devious mind of the empress. It had reached the point where even the most limited political foresight could predict Kantakouzenos' eventual victory. Anne herself apparently realized it was in the offing, and decided to be rid of the patriarch before Kantakouzenos' inevitable take-over, at which time Kalekas was sure to be deposed anyway. To accomplish her ends, Anne alleged that the patriarch's orthodoxy was questionable. In actuality, Anne cared next to nothing about orthodoxy. (Current gossip held that in spite of her baptism into the Orthodox faith she had secretly remained a Catholic.) Religion of any sort obviously had little real meaning for her, but having decided to depose Kalekas, she pursued this objective relentlessly until she contrived his removal.

On an evening in early February 1347, while Anne was holding a banquet at Blachernai Palace to celebrate the patriarch's ouster, frantic messengers burst into the hall with the news that collaborators had opened the walled-up Golden Gate to John Kantakouzenos, and that at that very moment his forces were making their way into the city.[7] The Emperor John VI had come to claim his capital. Anne laughed; these reports, she declared, were a mere ruse by the ex-patriarch to dampen her enjoyment of his fall. Anne's feasting and merrymaking, with crude jokes about her various foes, lasted far into the night. When she awoke the next morning it was to the reality that Kantakouzenos' men were in possession of most of the city. Within hours he would arrive at Blachernai Palace. Did the empress-mother wish to negotiate? Anne responded to Kantakouzenos' messenger with a veritable flood of coarse insults against her adversary, though with the news that his forces had actually broken into the palace, she agreed to meet with him and attempt to work out a settlement.

When Kantakouzenos arrived, he found that Anne had posted herself at the most impressive spot in the palace. With her young sons John and Michael, she stood beneath a large and holy icon of the Blessed Virgin. For all her pettiness, Anne could be regal when she had to be. She stood waiting now with her children, a sacrifice to be offered. Kantakouzenos approached, bowed solemnly, and kissed the hand of the fourteen-year-old Emperor John. He had not come, he said, to conquer, but to share the throne with the son of his friend.

Whatever Anne may have thought, young John reputedly wanted peace. Within a few days the details of the arrangement were worked out. Anne and her family kept Blachernai Palace. Kantakouzenos and his family moved into one of the older—and much decayed—imperial residences. Anne's name would still come first in all imperial proclamations, but all real decision-making power was vested in Kantakouzenos. For ten years, it was decided, he would rank as basileus and autokrator, after which he would continue as co-emperor but would yield precedence to young John V.[8] Kantakouzenos, who was naturally inclined to mercy, agreed readily to widespread amnesty for those who had supported Anne in the six-year war now ending.

In May, Kantakouzenos and Irene his wife were solemnly crowned in Blachernai Chapel. As if symbolic of the strife of Anne and Kantakouzenos, an earthquake some months earlier had destroyed one of the venerable domes of Hagia Sophia, and the great church, for centuries the traditional site of the coronation, could not be used. There was no money for repairs, and would not be for a long time. (A few years later, when the Grand Prince of Moscow sent a generous contribution for rebuilding, Kantakouzenos found it necessary to hand it over instead to his Turkish mercenaries.)[9]

As a part of the general celebration for Kantakouzenos coronation, another ceremony of vast significance was held in Blachernai Chapel: John V, aged fourteen, was married to the daughter of his new co-emperor. Helena Kantakouzene was also fourteen.

There were now two emperors and three empresses; peace had returned to the empire at last. But the jewels in the imperial crowns were bits of colored glass; the gold was actually gilded leather, and the vessels on the tables at the coronation banquet were of pewter, clay, and seashells.[10]

As time would prove, there was no real winner in the terrible strife of Anne and Kantakouzenos. For Byzantines of all classes the struggle had been one of unrelieved disaster. In the areas where fighting had raged the heaviest, the fields lay uncultivated, and thousands were dead— or dying—from simple lack of sufficient food. Thousands more had been slain indiscriminately by the Turkish and Serbian mercenaries employed by the warring contenders for power. Kantakouzenos' persistence had won him the throne of a dying empire. In the years that followed he would have ample opportunity to realize what a heavy burden was his crown of colored glass.

11

Crown of Colored Glass

Once secure in his possession of the empire, Kantakouzenos sincerely tried to improve Byzantium's desperate situation. The imperial treasury was empty; as one contemporary remarked, it contained "nothing but air and dust."[1] The devastated common folk obviously could return little—if any—revenues to the state; the nobles who had managed to survive the war and who controlled what wealth was still left in the Byzantine world stood on their ancient privileges of tax exemption. Kantakouzenos called delegations of them to the palace and pleaded eloquently for free-will contributions, but the returns were so disappointingly small that the emperor was obliged to impose extraordinary taxes in order to have the basis to begin one of his long-cherished dreams: the building up of a substantial Byzantine fleet.[2] As ships were constructed Kantakouzenos hopefully envisioned a gradual return of Byzantium's once-great maritime trade, and moved to impose new restrictions on the city's nearest and most dangerous commercial rival, the Genoese of Pera, who shared with Constantinople the harbor of the Golden Horn.

The outcome was inevitable. The angry Genoese were not about to submit to the new trade regulations. So many incidents took place between Genoese and Byzantine ships that the Golden Horn was rapidly becoming the scene of a full-scale war. Kantakouzenos appealed for—and with great difficulty collected—additional revenue for ship-building. But on the day when the new fleet was finally put to the test of an all-out assault on the Genoese, the results were disastrous for the inexperienced seamen newly recruited into the Byzantine navy. When the weather turned suddenly stormy, many of them panicked and jumped overboard, making no effort to fulfill their duties. The Genoese sailors, even as they seized the deserted Byzantine vessels and hauled them back to Pera's side of the harbor, could scarcely believe the ease with which they had defeated their enemies.[3]

The military disasters of the war with Pera were compounded by an even greater natural disaster early in Kantakouzenos' reign. Out of the East, from a Genoese colony on the Black Sea, came the dreadful epidemic of bubonic plague that people called the Black Death. It was estimated that in 1347 and 1348, as many as one-third of the inhabitants of Constantinople died of the fearful disease. Vast stretches of the city were abandoned, and would lie uninhabited for years to come. The plague was no respecter of persons, and among the dead was Kantakouzenos' youngest son, the little prince Andronikos.[4]

Staggered by this personal loss and by the many blows the empire was suffering, Kantakouzenos still persisted in his determination to set things right in Byzantium. Theology was one of the areas demanding his urgent concern, and typical Byzantine that he was, Kantakouzenos was ready to tackle religious disputes with a genuine fervor. The great controversy of the time centered around the claims of the Palamite faction, who had developed a peculiar discipline of meditation in quest of the inner light, the "heavenly light of Mount Tabor." Many of the Palamites (or Hesychasts) had supported Kantakouzenos in his struggle for the throne, and it was only to be expected that he would defend them from the charges of heresy levied against them by some of their opponents. Two councils on the subject were held in the summer of 1351, and Hesychasm was declared fully Orthodox.[5] This decision probably contributed to the growth of "otherworldliness" in Eastern monasticism for centuries to come.

A famous manuscript portrait[6] still exists depicting Kantakouzenos at one of the council meetings, surrounded by a host of bishops and other Orthodox dignitaries. The emperor sits enthroned in apparent splendor; his purple robe is bedecked with numerous (if synthetic) jewels; his red shoes rest on a magnificent red footstool on which the double eagles of the Palaiologos family are vividly displayed. (After all, Kantakouzenos was a Palaiologos, too, and he did not hesitate to use this imperial symbol.) Most interesting of all, however, is the aging emperor's face; the impassive, oriental features betray no hint of his lifetime of struggle. For all one could guess from the portrait, the dignified, grey-haired emperor with his elegant forked beard might well have spent his entire life secure in possession of the empire he had seized only at such great cost.

One may wonder if Kantakouzenos, even at the height of his power, reflected on the relative insecurity of his position. Perhaps it was hoping for the miraculous to expect young John V to remain content with his demotion to emperor of second rank. Not only in his astonishing good looks—his curly golden hair and fair skin, his completely un-Byzantine appearance—did John V resemble his mother Anne. Unfortunately his mind worked—or failed to work—altogether too much as hers did. He wanted power, though he scarcely knew why, or what to do with it.

Kantakouzenos, hoping to keep the young man profitably occupied, sent him to Thessaloniki to serve as provincial governor, and for the time being things seemed to be reasonably well settled.

By the time John and his wife Helena Kantakouzene

were eighteen, they were the parents of three children: Andronikos, Irene, and Manuel. Manuel was just a newborn baby when rumors began to drift back to the capital that John V was planning to divorce Helena in order to marry a sister of Stephen Dushan.[7] The Serbian tsar in recent years had continued his incursions into the Byzantine state and annexed considerable imperial territory to the Serbian realm. His enmity toward Kantakouzenos was among the gravest dangers facing the empire. Now, it appeared, young John was ready to abandon the mother of his heirs in return for Dushan's aid. The truth of this report, however, is difficult to determine. Divorce was never easy to obtain in the Orthodox world, and while John may have dangled the prospect of a marriage alliance before Dushan, it seems altogether unlikely that he seriously intended to carry through with it. Helena, for her part, was deeply devoted to her young husband. When Kantakouzenos summoned her back to the capital, she replied spiritedly, "Rather than live with my parents, I would die with John."

Perhaps Kantakouzenos was moved by his daughter's outspoken loyalty. In any event, he was determined if possible to stop any intrigues between his son-in-law and Dushan. Kantakouzenos discussed the whole matter with Anne; to preserve the peace and to assure that their children remained married to each other, Kantakouzenos vowed he was willing to give up his position as autokrator, and to convince Anne of his sincerity he swore an oath to this effect in the Blachernai Chapel. Anne agreed to go to Thessaloniki with the message.

Whatever his faults, John Kantakouzenos had a reputation for basic honesty. Even Anne seems to have believed him, yet it is also an unpleasant reality that this time he failed to live up to his word. It became amply clear to the young emperor and empress once they returned to Constantinople that Kantakouzenos was not about to hand over the post of autokrator to John V. Whether Kantakouzenos had deliberately perjured himself from the start is impossible to say. He may have sworn his oath with every intention of keeping it, and then when John was again in his presence, found the actual handing over of the empire to this shallow, immature, undisciplined youth simply more than he could bear. He did, however, extend John's governorship by assigning to him several towns in Thrace, including his old family stronghold of Didymoteichos.

In spite of these concessions, the younger man was gravely disillusioned with his father-in-law. With Helena and baby Manuel he returned to Thessaloniki, while the two older children, Andronikos and Irene, remained with their grandparents. This was a strange arrangement in view of the hostilities soon to come, but perhaps an indication, too, that whatever resentments lay between the generations, John and his young wife knew that her father was a basically decent man.

The new round of hostilities broke out in 1352. Though at first it seemed that the young emperor might make good his attempts to replace Kantakouzenos, the sudden death of Stephen Dushan dampened John's hopes for Serbian aid, and by 1353, John and Helena with little Manuel had fled to the dreary island of Tenedos.[8] Meanwhile in Constantinople, Kantakouzenos had his oldest son Matthias crowned as co-emperor,[9] an act that plainly demonstrated his complete break with John V and his new resolve to make the Kantakouzenos dynasty a permanent institution. For the time it seemed that the house of Palaiologos was fallen to rise no more.

Nevertheless, young John was as busy as ever with his intrigues. Ultimately, according to one report, he managed to win the support of a certain enterprising Genoese soldier of fortune, Francesco Gattilusi, who commanded a substantial following.[10] John V offered a tempting bargain: if Gattilusi could restore him to the imperial throne, John would give him the Island of Lesbos. Moreover, John's

young sister, Princess Maria, would become Gattilusi's
wife. The enterprising Francesco accepted the offer. John
and his Genoese allies attempted a naval attack on the
capital and failed miserably. Another round of the conflict
had come to an end.

Francesco Gattilusi, however, was undaunted. Still
determined to claim his prize, he calculated how he might
win by stratagem what their meager numbers could never
accomplish by force alone. On their next voyage to the
capital in November of 1354, Gattilusi made sure his ships
were loaded with a large supply of empty oil jars.

On the appointed date in the dead of the night, the
Genoese attacked. Inside the imperial palace, Kantakouzenos and the whole household were awakened by a great
furor outside the walls: loud, shattering sounds reverber-
ated through the chill November air. The emperor immediately sent men to investigate the disturbance—a noise
that sounded for all the world as if a host of many
thousands had attacked the capital.

The crashing sounds, it turned out, were being caused
by Gattilusi's men as they hurled their empty oil jars
against the palace walls. As Kantakouzenos' men came
down to investigate, the Genoese overpowered them, and
rushed through the gate. A desperate stratagem had paid
off: the Emperor John V was back in his capital.

Strangely enough, Kantakouzenos chose not to defend
himself. In the next few weeks, he met often with his son-
in-law and seemingly pleaded with him for a restoration of
their old imperial partnership. John V would have none of
it. In December, Kantakouzenos officially abdicated and
agreed to submit himself to the vows of monastic life. He
had long intended to end his days as a monk, in any event,
he alleged. Irene, his wife of many years, perhaps less
willingly agreed to become a nun. "If I had guarded
Didymoteichos as you have guarded Constantinople, we
should have said our farewells twelve years ago," she
reputedly remarked to her husband.[11] Be that as it may, the

farewells were said at last; and the imperial couple retired to their respective cloisters in Constantinople, he to Saint George of the Mangana Monastery, she to the Convent of Kyra Martha.[12]

Kantakouzenos' monastic life, however, was far from typical. In the monastery, according to the long standing custom, John Kantakouzenos took a new name: from now on he would be simply Brother Joasaph. Not long afterwards he moved from the Mangana to the Charianeites Monastery, also in Constantinople. There, determined to surround himself with at least some of his former comforts, he paid for renovations of the monastery. A loggia and balcony were built and extensive interior decoration provided at Brother Joasaph's expense.[13] In a sense, this monastic retreat would be for him a pleasant retirement home, where he might study and write and reflect upon the troubled course of his long life.

Whenever he pleased he was free to visit the outside world. There were occasional family reunions when he and his wife Irene—now Sister Evgenia—both left their cloisters and visited with the Kantakouzenos children.[14] Significantly, Brother Joasaph remained on good terms with his daughter, the Empress Helena, and it was probably through her good offices that he was soon again to be welcomed at the imperial palace. A strange peace pervaded the imperial household after the long years of strife among themselves. Kantakouzenos' sons, Matthias (who was finally compelled to renounce his title as co-emperor) and his younger brother Manuel (whom John V recognized as Despot of the Morea) lived in the Greek town of Mistra. This small outpost near the site of ancient Sparta served as capital of the Kantakouzenos appanage. The sons of the fallen emperor governed their territory as if it were an independent state and the Morea (the "Land of the Mulberries") flourished under their rule. Ironically, the division of the imperial territories so longed for by the Empress Yolande half a century before had now become a reality.

Henceforth, every emperor's son, regardless of his order of birth, would expect and generally would receive certain territories to govern on his own.

As for Brother Joasaph, he was of course a monk and must remain so forever, yet as a respected elder statesman and advisor to his son-in-law, John V, he again spoke in the councils of empire. The Patriarch Philotheos summarized Kantakouzenos' new position clearly when he reported: "Formerly his subordinates bowed before him because he was their master, but everyone did not do so with sincerity. Today everyone does so sincerely, with good will and love. . . . All the imperial family love him as children love their father." John V himself reportedly spoke of his father-in-law as "the prop of his throne, a divine councilor, the soul of his policy, of his life, his empire, and that of his children."[15] They did not always agree, particularly on religious matters, but Brother Joasaph was listened to and he knew his opinions counted for a great deal. Although Orthodox monks were supposed to claim no surname, in due time he came to sign himself as the Emperor Brother Joasaph Kantakouzenos.[16] Who could blame him? It was a small thing—and yet it constituted recognition of the fact that though he was bound by irrevocable monastic vows, he was also in a sense irrevocably an emperor; his consecration as basileus had conferred upon him a special character as indelible as that of a monk.

As for Anne of Savoy, Kantakouzenos' great adversary, ironically she, too, may have ended her days in the religious life. Considerable mystery surrounds the later life of the Empress Anne. According to one report she returned to the Roman Catholic faith of her early youth and became a Franciscan nun in Italy, but this is far from certain. Another report has it that she spent her last years in Thessaloniki. The exact date of her death is unknown.[17]

Meanwhile John—or Joasaph—Kantakouzenos lived to a ripe old age in his monastic retreat in Constantinople.

Sometimes he spoke of moving to one of the remote and intensely ascetic cloisters on Mount Athos, but he never did. [18] His interest in the active world of politics was still too strong. He gladly assisted John V whenever he could, and he also found considerable time to devote to theological study. Besides his religious writings, he composed a history of his life and reign. As is only to be expected, he tried to make himself appear in the best possible light. He was well up into his eighties when, as will be seen, he was taken prisoner by his grandson, Andronikos IV. For two years the aged man was held in custody under wretched conditions in Pera, but he lived to see his son-in-law, his one-time bitter foe John V, return to set him free.

Kantakouzenos decided after this to retire from the capital; his son Matthias offered him a home in Mistra, and the old emperor-monk retired gratefully to the quiet provincial town. There on the fifteenth of June, 1383, forty-two years to the day since the death of his "spiritual brother" Andronikos III, Kantakouzenos died. He was eighty-eight years old—the greatest age of any sovereign in the long roll of the Byzantine emperors.

A historian of the time pronounced what is perhaps the fairest verdict upon him: he might have been "a very great emperor, capable of bringing the empire to unparalleled prosperity"[19] if only he had lived in a happier era.

12

John the Son of Anne

John V was twenty-two when with the aid of Gattilusi and the empty oil jars he made good his claim to the imperial throne and Kantakouzenos was finally brought to terms. John's future, however, was to be anything but peaceful.[1] The long reign of this well-meaning but sadly incompetent sovereign is a tapestry of intrigue and counter-plot, of Palaiologoi warring among themselves while the empire's territories gradually passed into the hands of the Ottoman Turks. It is a dismal tale on the whole; looking back from the vantage point of centuries, one finds it easy to despise the petty Byzantine princelings whose personal ambitions contributed in such large measure to their empire's fall. Yet it is not an account of unrelieved disaster. If John V was unfortunate in practically everything he undertook, he had at least one son, Manuel, who served him faithfully through almost all his trials. Manuel's integrity and his deep and genuine devotion both to his father and to the Byzantine state come like a refreshing breeze in the midst of the disheartening intrigues of John V's world.

Manuel was the third of the five children of John V and Helena Kantakouzene. Andronikos, the eldest, had arrived in 1348 when his father was not quite sixteen.[2] The next year witnessed the birth of the little princess, Irene and then on June 27, 1350, Manuel was born. Two more sons, Theodore and Michael, born a few years later, completed the family.

In one of his letters written long thereafter, Manuel presents an interesting glimpse of the princes' early education. He was himself a bookish lad and preferred to devote his time to literary studies "with the aim of surpassing all the learned." But, he goes on, "according to a decision of the council, other studies followed one upon the other and I was compelled to alternate between many teachers each day, who taught a number of different subjects; how to handle the bow and spear and how to ride a horse."[3] While Manuel may not have enjoyed these athletic pursuits to the extent that he enjoyed reading, he was a strong and healthy young man and proved completely capable in the military arts.

Manuel and his elder brother Andronikos grew up as different as two sons of the same father could possibly be. Andronikos was a restless intriguer with little regard for those he must trample in his quest to have what he wanted; Manuel was scholarly and patient, and deeply devoted to his family. Since Manuel was not the first-born, in the ordinary course of events he would have had little chance of inheriting the throne. The course of events in late fourteenth-century Byzantium, however, would prove to be anything but ordinary. As Andronikos grew to manhood he made little effort to conceal his contempt for his bumbling father John, his intellectual brother Manuel, or anyone else who posed a threat to his own exercise of power. Andronikos wanted the throne, and he wanted it as soon as possible. Perhaps the fact that John was so young, that there was a mere fifteen years between him and his first-born, augmented Andronikos' impatience. In any event, when the Emperor John embarked on a journey to Italy leaving twenty-one-year-old Andronikos as co-emperor and regent, the young man was delighted. The longer his father stayed away, the better he would like it.

Meanwhile the Emperor John toured Italy in a futile attempt to secure allies for Byzantium, and at length came to Rome where he took the final step in his quest for support from Western Christendom. Pope Urban V, who was duly forewarned of the important plans that John Palaiologos had in mind, journeyed from his palatial residence in Avignon to meet the emperor in Rome. There in a great public ceremony, John was received as a convert into the Roman Catholic Church. A few days later, standing on the steps of St. Peter's, the Byzantine emperor made a public statement disavowing the "errors" of his former Greek Orthodox faith.[4]

John's conversion was a decision he had contemplated for a long time before making the irrevocable commitment. For some years he had been in correspondence with papal headquarters. In the course of these negotiations the emperor had once suggested some years earlier that he might send his little son Manuel to the papal court in Avignon to be reared as a Catholic in return for financial aid from the papacy, an idea which apparently did not interest the pope at all.[5] Then in 1366, John had undertaken a futile journey to Hungary in search of Western aid, the first Byzantine emperor ever to appear as a suppliant at a foreign court. The Hungarian King Lajos informed him outright that if he hoped for any kind of Western assistance against the Ottoman Turks, he would have to accept Roman Catholicism. To John V the theological differences that so aroused some Orthodox believers mattered little. He had postponed taking the final step as long as he did mainly because his father-in-law Kantakouzenos was so opposed to it. Now, in Rome, he was determined to postpone it no longer.

The news of their emperor's conversion came to many Byzantines as a shocking and unwelcome surprise. To them it seemed an unpatriotic betrayal of the faith of their fathers; a cheap trick with no other motive than the obtaining of highly dubious allies. But at least it was understood it was his own personal decision: he was not going to try to force union on all the Orthodox as his ancestor Michael VIII had done. From John's viewpoint, the matter must have appeared in a different light. He cannot have resented the Roman church as most Byzantines did; he was half-Italian himself; his mother Anne had been a Catholic. Of course he wanted Western aid, but he may also have believed that his acceptance of Catholicism would form a bridge of understanding between East and West.

As usual, John V was mistaken. The pope, though he made an appeal for volunteers to assist Byzantium, was beset by cares closer home and was in no position actually to aid the Byzantine state in its struggle for survival. Nor were other Western princes eager to take up arms on behalf of the emperor of the East merely because he had become a Catholic. To John's credit, however, it must be added (even if it was to the dismay of his subjects) that as long as he lived, he would remain a practicing Roman Catholic.

It is easy to imagine how young Andronikos, back in Constantinople, reacted to the news of his father's change of religion: now more than ever he could feel smugly self-righteous in his resentment of parental authority. Meanwhile, the Emperor John, blissfully unaware of these growing problems at home, continued his Italian travels in Naples and Ancona, and at last sailed to Venice. There he hoped to obtain financial assistance and to redeem those crown jewels pawned to the Venetians by his mother Anne some years before. Unfortunately, the emperor was already heavily in debt to the Venetian Republic and now that he was bodily present in the city, his creditors believed that they had their golden opportunity to press for repayment of his earlier loans plus interest. There is considerable conflict in the sources as to the treatment John received in Venice.[6] While it is clear that the Venetians did not toss the Byzantine emperor into a common debtors' prison and in fact seem to have accorded him the usual privileges of visiting royalty, his sojourn could not have been a pleasant experience. Moreover, he was growing so embarrassingly short of funds that without help he could not even provision ships for the homeward voyage to Constantinople. John sent a frantic appeal to his son Andronikos.

Andronikos' reply was vague and altogether unhelpful: he had insufficient funds himself and could not obtain more without requisitioning treasures from the Orthodox Church, and certainly he would not do that! It was obvious that the ambitious young co-emperor had no desire to see his father set free. It is at this point that the Prince Manuel first appears as an important figure on the political scene. In his late teens, Manuel had been appointed Despot of Thessaloniki, and from this city he now set sail to rescue John from Venice. He brought with him what resources he had available (it seems he did not hesitate to borrow from the church). Though he by no means possessed the funds the Venetians sought, he was prepared to offer himself as a hostage in his father's place. The Despot of Thessaloniki was a persuasive young man, and after some weeks of negotiation, the Venetian state agreed to let John go. The cost was heavy; the cession of the important island of Tenedos to Venice was agreed upon,[7] as well as Manuel's continued presence in Venice, but at least the emperor was able to return to Constantinople. The humiliating crisis had subsided and before another year passed, John arranged to get Manuel home again. Although Andronikos was still officially co-emperor and heir to the throne, it was obvious from this time on that Manuel was John's favorite son.

Andronikos II Palaiologos
Manuscript miniature. Cod. Monacensis Gr. 442
Staatsbibliothek, Munich

Andronikos III Palaiologos
Manuscript miniature. Cod. Hist. F. 601, f.2
Landesbibliothek, Stuttgart

Anne of Savoy
Manuscript miniature. Cod. Hist. F. 601, f.4
Landesbibliothek, Stuttgart

**John Kantakouzenos as emperor
and as Brother Joasaph**
Manuscript miniature. Cod. Gr. 1242, f.123v.
Bibliothèque Nationale, Paris

**John V Palaiologos (left) with his son
Manuel II (center)
and grandson John VIII (right)**
Pen and ink sketch. Cod. Gr. 1783, f.2
Bibliothèque Nationale, Paris

Andronikos IV Palaiologos
Manuscript miniature. Cod. d.S.5.5.
Biblioteca Estense, Modena

Manuel II Palaiologos
Manuscript miniature. Cod. Sup. Gr. 309, f.6
Bibliothèque Nationale, Paris

John VIII Palaiologos
Bronze medal by Pisanello
The British Museum, London

13

The Windowless Tower

Andronikos was largely responsible for his own troubles, but like many another young person at odds with his family, by this time he could envision no practical course of action but further rebellion. His webs of intrigue grew more complicated even as Byzantium's political situation vis à vis the Ottoman Turks grew progressively darker. These were years of rapid Ottoman expansion at Byzantine expense, until the territories under the rule of the empire were so reduced that John V was compelled to recognize the Sultan Murad as his overlord and render him tribute lest his realm be totally demolished. John was even required on several occasions to serve personally as an officer in the sultan's army and to bring with him a small force of Byzantine men-at-arms. To help the Turks in carving out an empire from lands that had once been Byzantine was a terrible humiliation; but failing the arrival of those Western allies whom he never ceased to hope for, it was all that John V could do.

It was against this background that a few years after John's return from Venice, the worthless Andronikos plotted his father's fall.[1] The Turkish Prince Saudji, son of Murad, he discovered, was like himself restless under parental authority. The Byzantine prince and the Turkish one agreed to join forces and war was launched against their respective fathers.

As it turned out, however, the uprising of the princes was crushed. For his rebellious son, the Sultan Murad decreed blinding—inflicted in such a manner that the Turkish prince died. John V, the sultan added, must see to it that Andronikos received a similar sentence; not necessarily death, but certainly the deprivation of his eyesight.

John Palaiologos' heart must have shaken like a tree in a windstorm. To disobey his overlord was unthinkable, but to mutilate his son was something terrible to contemplate. Wild, restless rebel Andronikos might be, but he was John's first-born and John apparently still loved him. Nonetheless, the sultan had commanded, and (according to some sources) had added that Andronikos' little son John, an infant just learning to talk, must meet the same penalty.[2]

And the sentence was carried out.[3]

Immediately thereafter, Andronikos and his family were whisked away to the Tower of Anemas, a dreary old prison built into the city wall beside Blachernai Palace. Not many weeks afterward, it was widely rumored that Prince Andronikos and his baby son had recovered their sight.[4] Andronikos' wife, Maria-Kyratza Asen, it was whispered, possessed a wonder-working salve which she rubbed on the eyelids of the victims. The whole incident is full of the aura of mystery that Byzantines through the centuries loved so well. What really happened is impossible to say, yet one strongly suspects that although Andronikos' eyesight may have been damaged, especially in one eye, the blinding irons or basins used on John V's rebellious offspring were never intended to do a thorough job and that the wondrous "recovery" was neatly preplanned. Not even the sultan of the Turks could countermand a miracle.

Andronikos, however, did not get off scot-free. While he might rejoice over the "recovery" of his eyesight, his father and the sultan agreed that he must be deprived of his right to the imperial succession. Thus Manuel was named heir to the throne in his brother's place, while Andronikos languished in his tower with ample time to reflect on the folly that had cost him so dear and to plan revenge should ever he regain his freedom.

According to one tale that was still being circulated in Constantinople years later, Andronikos' imprisonment was finally terminated as the result of a strange incident.[5] One day Maria-Kyratza spied a snake of "marvelous bigness" creeping out of a hole in the wall of the cell she shared with her husband, and then disappearing back into its hiding place. When it emerged again, Andronikos strangled the serpent with his bare hands, and had it sent to his father—a token of the fearful living conditions in his prison. If this report be a true one, John V was moved to such compassion that he released his son then and there. More likely, however, though the circumstances of the prince's confinement may have softened at this point, he did not actually regain his freedom until he contrived to take refuge with the Genoese of Pera. It was the summer of 1376.

Events moved rapidly in the weeks that followed. The Sultan Murad, so recently Andronikos' deadly foe, was always willing to play the game of fomenting trouble among the Palaiologoi and promised his support for the fugitive prince, while the Genoese of Pera were eager to assist anyone who promised a change from John V's pro-Venetian policy. Thus with Genoese and Turkish forces to back him up, Andronikos reasserted his claim to the Byzantine throne. For about a month, his troops besieged Constantinople, at length forcing entrance into the city. For many days thereafter, fighting raged in the streets, but in time Andronikos emerged victorious. The prize he so longed for was in his grasp; he was the Basileus and Autokrator Andronikos IV. His father John was his prisoner; so was his brother Manuel, who had been severely wounded in the course of the fighting, and another brother, Theodore. Andronikos apparently had nothing against Theodore and was willing to let him go; but for John and Manuel his decree was imprisonment in a windowless cell in the Tower of Anemas. Both the Emperor John and Manuel, it is reported, pleaded with Theodore to avail himself of the opportunity for freedom, but the young man refused to desert them, particularly since Manuel was wounded.[6]

The Palaiologoi were a family of intense feelings. The brotherly loyalty of Manuel and Theodore was as strong as Andronikos' hatred and would always be so. Though in later years the two would go their separate ways and see little of each other, one senses something of the bond between them when Manuel describes Theodore not only as his favorite brother but his "dearest friend."[7]

Though Manuel's wounds healed under Theodore's devoted care, the long months in the windowless tower passed slowly for the imperial prisoners. "Many ills visited us and caused us bitter and deep suffering," Manuel recalled later. "Since as far as reason could see, there was no hope of being freed, the situation compelled us to hate life itself."

In their enforced withdrawal, Manuel devoted himself to scholarship with new fervor and in this way, as he wrote later, he was able to dispel the "cloud of despondency" that hung over him. "It seemed good to me to take as my continuous activity a preoccupation with books, nightly and by day," Manuel recollected in a letter written years thereafter. "But then, why do I say 'by day'? There it was eternally a gloomy night. . . . Anyone who turned to such occupation was obliged to use a lantern. Our prison cut off the rays of high noon as effectively as, elsewhere on earth, night cuts them off from those who are outside of prison. Being destitute of any instructor, I was not able to advance in proportion to my many labors. . . . Nevertheless . . . in the very continuity of my activity an utterly tyrannical desire for my studies sank deeply into my soul. Thus has it altogether prevailed, so as to make me not merely a devotee of this activity, but an extreme fanatic."[8]

Theodore, like Manuel, was intellectually minded, and the two brothers whiled away the hours with their rhetorical and philosophical disputations. Manuel developed an elegant literary style, rather too verbose for modern tastes but with the rhetorical polish that so delighted the intelligentsia of the late Byzantine world. The intense boredom of John V, captive audience for his sons' scholarly exercises, can only be imagined. He was no scholar and never had been. His sons, it was obvious, were more Kantakouzenos than Palaiologos—philosophers like their old grandfather John Kantakouzenos, who had given up his throne and who lived yet, writing his books and meditating, perhaps, on the folly of political intrigue. The months stretched into years, and in their dark cell John V and his sons awaited the future with uncertainty.

Of course, they plotted to escape. Manuel, had he had a mind to, could have told us a great deal about these schemes which must have formed an exciting chapter in his life. Apparently, however, it was never a subject he would discuss freely, so the details of how he and his family came to leave the Tower of Anemas remain to this day a mystery.

According to one account written by a Venetian historian some years later, John V (who was always something of a ladies' man) seduced the wife of the jailer, and she in turn promised to serve as go-between to smuggle letters from John to a Venetian adventurer, Carlo Zeno.[9] Zeno agreed to attempt the emperor's rescue, approached the tower by boat, and climbed in through a window. These details are not completely accurate, for the Tower of Anemas was built into the landward wall of Constantinople, and Manuel stresses the fact that the cell he shared with his father and brother was windowless. Still, the daring Zeno may have contacted the imperial captives in some way, for the account goes on to relate how he urged John to flee away with him that very night. In tears, John refused, thanking Zeno profusely for his brave effort, but declaring that he would not desert his sons, for he feared that great harm would be done to them if he should escape and they be left behind. The breakaway was consequently postponed, and in the days that followed, John again employed his mistress to carry messages to Zeno and his Venetians. The unfortunate woman, however, was found out by Maria-Kyratza, who was serving as regent while her husband Andronikos IV was away on a journey. Maria ordered the poor woman tortured and thus extorted from her the details of the intrigue. The outcome of these events, which occurred in the early weeks of their confinement, must have left the imperial prisoners more despondent than ever.

It was almost three years before they made good their plans to escape. Almost certainly Venetians were involved in this scheme as in the earlier attempt to free the imperial prisoners. It is highly probable, too, that Helena Kantakouzene, John's wife, played an important role in the escape.[10] In any case, we do know that on leaving the windowless tower, John, Manuel, and Theodore fled for refuge to the court of Sultan Murad himself. The sultan, they had reason to believe, no longer found Andronikos a tool to his liking. As willing as ever to stir up trouble among the Palaiologoi, Murad agreed to place John back on the imperial throne.

With Turkish and Venetian aid, John re-entered Constantinople. But Andronikos was by no means ready to give up his throne. Though he fled from the capital, he removed only so far as Pera, the stronghold of his Genoese allies. Moreover, he took with him valuable hostages: his mother, the Empress Helena, her two sisters, and their father, the monk Kantakouzenos, who was well up into his eighties. Andronikos' ruthlessness is never more clearly seen than in his treatment of his mother, his aunts, and his grandfather; they were confined in cells in a fortress where plague cases had been reported, deprived of sufficient food, and placed in the care of rough, uncouth guards.[11] John V, Manuel, and their Venetian allies next besieged Pera intermittently for some months. Though the exact course of events is far from clear, John at length was compelled to submit to arbitration in order to secure release of the hostages. Andronikos agreed to lay down his arms provided he would again be recognized as his father's heir. The hostages would be freed. Theodore would depart for the Morea where he would rule as a semi-independent despot. It was an arrangement whereby everyone stood to benefit except Manuel and for the time being it was the best John V could hope for. Manuel, who had shared his father's imprisonment for three years, who had fought for him and who genuinely loved him, was now nothing; Andronikos the rebel, who felt only contempt for his father, was again co-emperor and heir apparent to the throne.

14

Manuel's "New Empire"

For Manuel the entire situation could not have been more dismal. In his disillusionment, the prince, who was now in his early thirties, decided upon a rash departure from his long course of faithful service to his father. Suddenly and without revealing his intentions to any of his family, Manuel disappeared from the imperial court, taking with him a small body of loyal troops. Within a short while, word reached Constantinople that the prince and his followers had arrived in Thessaloniki, the second city of the empire, and that Manuel had had himself recognized there as basileus. Manuel's Thessaloniki adventure was not rebellion against John; even in his grave disappointment, he would never seek to deprive his father of his crown. It was rather an assertion of his belief that since everything in Constantinople had turned out so badly, he was determined to make a new start elsewhere. He could legally claim Thessaloniki as his appanage by terms of his earlier appointment as despot of that city, and now from this base he would have the freedom to undertake a new offensive against the Turks while conveniently ignoring the fact that his father John was a sworn vassal of the sultan. Manuel was still young enough to believe in victory, idealistic enough to dream of a rebirth of Byzantium's past greatness.

In the weeks that followed Manuel's departure for Thessaloniki, rumors of his objectives drifted back to Constantinople and a considerable number of patriotic and adventurous young men left the capital to take service with the Basileus of Thessaloniki. In several encounters with Turkish forces in 1382-83, the troops of Manuel's "New Empire" were victorious. For about a year, it seemed, fortune favored the Byzantines, but this first flush of success was not destined to endure. By the autumn of 1383, the Turks had taken the Byzantine town of Serres, near Thessaloniki, and a few weeks later, the sultan's troops began to besiege the strongly walled city of Thessaloniki itself.

Because the city's location on the sea coast rendered it possible still to obtain supplies and reinforcements from outside, Manuel was by no means ready to despair at the outset of the Turkish siege. For three and a half years the city was to hold out before its inevitable fall.

While Manuel's Thessaloniki adventure dragged on to its tragic conclusion, back in Constantinople John V faced a new problem. Andronikos, it appeared, was still the restless intriguer he had always been. By 1385, warfare had again broken out between the emperor and his eldest son. A scribal note appended to a copy of their earlier treaty tells the story succinctly: "Know that not only were the above articles not observed, but the aforesaid Emperor Lord Andronikos took one fortress and the Lord Emperor John went forth in order to defend his territory. And Andronikos advanced against his father with his whole force and God preserved the Lord Emperor John from the wrath and evil intent of his son."[1]

Andronikos, temporarily defeated, withdrew to his stronghold of Selymbria. No doubt he was planning further hostilities when in June of 1385 he suddenly fell ill and died. He was only thirty-seven; but in his short lifetime he had contributed probably more than any of the Palaiologoi to the empire's final collapse.

With Andronikos' death, the question of the imperial succession was by no means resolved. Andronikos' son, Prince John, was a young man in his late teens, and would no doubt attempt sooner or later to press his claim to the throne. Yet there were also influential friends of Manuel at the old emperor's court who saw this as the ideal time to revive Manuel's claim, and who urged him to leave Thessaloniki, which was sure to fall anyway, and to seek his father's pardon. "Only return," wrote Manuel's friend and former tutor, Kydones, "and show that you have decided to submit to your father, the emperor, and that you are willing to obey his commands. . . . He will surpass the expectations of all in his generosity towards you."[2] Manuel must be prepared, Kydones added, to bring back only a small entourage with him; such was John's only apparent demand for reconciliation.

Manuel, still refusing to abandon Thessaloniki, received these pleas but did not stir. So long as there was even a faint hope of aid for the beleaguered city, he intended to remain with the task at hand. He sent appeals to his brother Theodore, Despot of the Morea, but Theodore, beset by military crises nearer home, was powerless to help. Intensely Orthodox though he was, Manuel also appealed to Pope Urban VI, but this attempt likewise proved a false hope. (The Great Schism of the West was by this time at the height of its fury, and Pope Urban of Rome was fully occupied trying to cope with his rival Pope Clement of Avignon.)

Finally in the spring of 1387, Manuel and his troops departed from Thessaloniki by sea at the insistence of the townspeople, who could endure the hardships of the siege no longer. The local government officials then surrendered the city to the Turks.

Many people expected at this point that Manuel would return to Constantinople to make his peace with his father.

The defeated prince decided rather to seek refuge on the Island of Lesbos, ruled by the Gattilusi family, cousins and old friends of the Palaiologoi. If he had been willing to abandon his followers to their fate, he might have returned to his father's court at once, but this was something Manuel could not do. For weeks he and the volunteers who had fought for him at Thessaloniki were lodged in small, uncomfortable tents beneath the scorching summer sun outside the city walls of Mitylene. During this time, Manuel was clearly involved in negotiations to smooth the way for his and their return to John V's good graces.

Though Manuel's mother, Helena Kantakouzene, seems to have pleaded with John to allow his return, and though John himself was reputedly kindly disposed towards Manuel, it seems that the emperor's advisors urged him to pursue a hard-line policy against the exiled prince. Two years passed before he was finally allowed to come home to Constantinople, once more to be recognized as co-emperor and heir to the throne. It is hard to understand why John was so slow to receive back the son who was, in reality, his staunchest ally, but Manuel at least seemed to harbor no ill feelings. Years later he wrote of his father: John was "a most excellent basileus, who displayed great affection to his sons."[3]

It was 1389 or 1390 that Manuel returned to his father's court. When he was nearly forty, Manuel's youth was fading; streaks of grey had appeared in his hair and beard, and he looked for all the world almost as old as his father John. He had never married. Not that he hated women—the existence of his little daughter Zampia and one or two other illegitimate offspring was proof against that. But it simply had not been possible to find a suitable bride for a Byzantine princeling of such uncertain future. And now, when his future seemed secure, came more trouble, more intrigue, more dissension among the Palaiologoi.

Prince John, the young son of Andronikos IV, who for

many months seems to have been living in distant Genoa[4] and apparently minding his own business, suddenly returned to Byzantium proclaiming his determination to keep the crown in the elder line of the family, though it meant rebellion against his grandfather John V.[5] The young man would be John VII (Kantakouzenos, after all, was John VI). By strict adherence to the law of primogeniture, John VII's claim to the throne was, of course, valid, but even though his coup had the backing of the Genoese and the new Turkish Sultan Bayazid, his tenure of the crown proved to be short. For five months in the spring and summer of 1390, while his grandfather remained holed up in the fortress at the Golden Gate, John VII reigned as basileus and autokrator. He blustered about, proclaiming how he intended to change his name from John to Andronikos (for after all, he did not wish to bear the same name as the grandfather who was his mortal enemy).[6] It was no use; the Byzantines continued to call him John. Nor was the young man any more successful in any of his other aspirations; he could only hope to be a tool in the hands of Sultan Bayazid, and it was widely rumored that the sultan was finding him less than satisfactory in this position.

In September 1390, with Bayazid's approval, John V was restored as emperor. It was Manuel who rescued his father as he had done so often before, though on the condition that he must go himself as a hostage to the Turks, a pledge of his father's continued submission to the sultan's overlordship. Manuel bore the humiliation as he had to, preserving toward the Turks an outward façade of serenity while he gave vent to his emotions in writing. With his Turkish captors he rode on campaign into the vast heart of Asia Minor and saw the lands that were the heritage of his forebears, now lost to Byzantium forever. Manuel knew the history of his people, and the reality of their former greatness and present misery touched him deeply.

In the course of these campaigns, the Turkish hosts

occasionally passed ruins where some great city of the Byzantines had stood in earlier times. "To my question what were the names of those cities," Manuel wrote later, "those whom I asked answered: 'As we have destroyed them, so time has destroyed their names,' and immediately sorrow seized me; but I sorrow silently, being still able to conceal my feelings."[7]

At home, John V, prematurely aged and afflicted with gout, perched precariously on the throne he had lost three times and three times regained, and dreamed of grandeur in his declining years. He would restore the crumbling fortifications of the capital city; and work was ordered to begin. Then came word from the Sultan Bayazid: pull down what you have built up or Manuel's eyes will be put out. For John V it was the final humiliation. He gave orders for demolition of his new construction, and died.[8]

A romantic but altogether unfounded tale circulated in later generations tells of the Emperor John dying in the arms of his young wife, Eudokia Komnene, widow of a Turkish lord.[9] This story, which has found its way into many history books, is completely false: the lady in question never existed.[10] Whatever his indiscretions (and John had certainly had his share of these), he died still married to Helena Kantakouzene, who had been his child bride more than forty years before. Helena, daughter, wife, and mother of emperors, followed the usual custom for imperial widows and became a nun—Sister Hypomene—soon after her husband's death. She died several years later.

John Palaiologos was fifty-eight years old at the time of his death. For fifty of those years he had borne the imperial title even if he had not always enjoyed the power that went with it. His was the longest reign in Byzantine history and beyond a doubt one of the most disastrous.

15

"Appear, Appear, Appear!"

When he learned of his father's death, Manuel somehow escaped the Turks and arrived home with lightning speed. At the age of forty, he was emperor at last—Manuel II, handsome, learned, and dignified, a true "philosopher king." Even his foes the Turks admitted Manuel's good looks, and one of them once paid him the supreme compliment of remarking that he bore a strong resemblance to the prophet Muhammad. As Manuel grew older, his long hair and beard, which had probably been blond, turned snow-white; and though he was rather short, his person emanated such dignity that "from the very sight of him alone, one was prompted to say, 'This man must be a king.' "[1]

Still Manuel's empire was one of the smallest states in Christendom. To hope for a reversal of the situation would have been unrealistic in the extreme. The new basileus realized that he was not called to be a conqueror but a preserver, to save what little was left and hand it on to his descendants.

To provide such heirs was one of Manuel's first concerns after his succession to the imperial throne. Now at last he was free to marry, and he chose as his bride Helena Dragases, a lady much younger than he, daughter of

Serbian warlord, Constantine Dragases. Manuel seems to have been entirely devoted to her and we hear of no other women in his life from this time forward.[2]

At the time of his marriage to Helena in February 1392, Manuel, who had been crowned as co-emperor by his father John years before, underwent a second coronation together with his young bride. An eyewitness account of the ceremonies reveals the Byzantines still delighting in the pageantry of bygone centuries and able to put on a brave show of limited magnificence.[3] According to the age-old practice, Manuel was raised upon a shield before his subjects, then conducted into the Church of Hagia Sophia. With bowed head, he stood before the patriarch, who besought God "send down Your power from Your holy abode through my sinful hands and anoint Your servant Manuel emperor and ruler of us, Your faithful people: bring forth in his days justice and the fulness of peace, subdue beneath his feet all foreign people who desire war. . . ."

After this optimistic prayer and chanted responses of "Holy, Holy, Holy" by the attendant clergy and "all the people," the patriarch anointed Manuel with holy oil, placed a crown on his head and a ceremonial cross in his right hand. Next Helena approached and bowed her head before her husband, while Manuel crowned her with the "crown customary for empresses" and handed her a golden scepter ornamented with jewels.

The long ceremony continued with the choir chanting praises to the newly consecrated sovereigns; then followed prayers, readings from the scriptures, and the receiving of Holy Communion by the emperor. When the services were concluded, Manuel and Helena rode back to the imperial palace. Everyone else walked, the high nobles vying with each other for the privilege of guiding the bridles of the imperial horses.

At the palace, the emperor and his bride mounted a podium and disappeared behind curtains of scarlet cloth, while the choir masters chanted, "Appear, appear, appear, rulers of the Romans!" At a given signal the curtains opened and Manuel and Helena, seated upon their imperial thrones, were revealed to the delighted gaze of their subjects. Then, after a little while, the scarlet curtains were drawn shut again. While Manuel and Helena proceeded with their nobles into the imperial dining hall for the coronation banquet, the grand chamberlain attended to a final ceremony still retained from Byzantium's more splendid centuries. Having ascended a "high place," presumably a platform specially constructed for the occasion, he tossed down to the crowds "little bundles" of coins wrapped in scraps of red silk, each bundle containing three pieces of gold, three of silver, and three of bronze. We are not informed how many of these packets were distributed, but in view of Manuel's perennial shortage of funds, his liberality must have been limited.

Within ten months after their marriage, Manuel and Helena were the parents of a son. The boy was named John according to the inevitable custom of bestowing upon the first-born son the name of his paternal grandfather. He later became the Emperor John VIII.

A charming manuscript miniature painted several years later presents a delightful glimpse of Manuel and his Serbian Helena and their growing family—by this time there were three sons.[4] The emperor and empress are clad in the stiff brocaded robes of the court, their faces serenely aristocratic beneath their heavy imperial crowns. Prince John, at his father's side, is dressed in a purple robe exactly like Manuel's, while the younger boys, Theodore and Andronikos, are wrapped from shoulders to toes in red cloaks emblazoned in gold with the Palaiologos double-eagle.

With the passing of years, Helena presented Manuel with a total of six sons who reached maturity and perhaps several daughters as well. There is considerable uncertainty as to the existence or the number of girls, for no clear record has come down to us. Manuel, who was forty-two when his first son John was born, was fifty-nine when the youngest, Thomas, arrived.[5]

But however blessed Manuel may have been in the number of his offspring, his good fortune was not so abundant in other areas. The early part of Manuel's reign proved, in fact, an intense struggle for Byzantium's survival. Manuel was at first willing to follow his father's conciliatory policy towards the Turks and even to present himself personally for service in Bayazid's army when called upon to do so. Apparently, however, the sultan was not satisfied with this arrangement and dreamed of plans for the total absorption of the Byzantine state.

The crisis reached the boiling point in 1394 when Bayazid summoned the Christian princes of southeastern Europe to a conference at Serres.[6] Manuel arrived in good faith, as did his brother, Theodore, Despot of Morea. They little realized that the sultan's intention was not to confer but to slay all his Christian vassals at one convenient time. The treacherous plot would have succeeded if the sultan's henchman who had been instructed to do the job had not stalled for time. Then at the last moment, Bayazid changed his mind. Still the act of near treachery was enough to prove the insecurity of Byzantium's position. From this time on, Manuel was committed to a policy of resistance to the Turks.

Not long after the Serres conference, the sultan began his siege of Constantinople—a semiblockade which was maintained for several years. Though the Turk would not take the Byzantine capital and at length abandoned his direct efforts to do so, practically everything outside the city walls fell into Turkish hands. During this time of crisis, Manuel secured the services of a few Western knights; among them was a French mercenary captain, Marshal Jean Boucicaut. While battling the Turks with indifferent success, Boucicaut conceived a plan for obtaining more Western aid and thereby saving the empire:

Manuel must go in person to the kings of Western Europe and explain to them Byzantium's need.

The emperor listened carefully to the appeals of the Frenchman. If the mercenary captain's speech lacked the rhetorical polish so dear to Manuel's heart, his message was clear nonetheless; the emperor must offer himself for this journey to the end of the earth. It might be Byzantium's last hope.

Manuel must have remembered his father's journey to Italy and its disastrous outcome many years before. Unlike John V, Manuel could not bear the thought of abandoning his Orthodox faith. If Boucicaut thought he was going to convert to Roman Catholicism, he had better think again. Still, Byzantium's best hope lay in the West. Not Italy, but France, as Marshal Boucicaut pointed out time and again—France was the rising star of the Westlands. Under the young King Charles VI, the nation that in centuries past had given birth to the greatest of the crusaders would have a new burst of glory.

Slowly but surely, Manuel began to be convinced. A great obstacle to his departure, however, was his nephew, the ex-emperor John VII, who had reigned for a few months in 1390 and who now lived in semi-exile in Selymbria, still coveting the throne. Manuel had attempted several years earlier to come to terms with John VII. The younger man, however, ever hopeful of a shift of fortunes whereby he might regain his throne, had refused his uncle's overtures to peace and preferred the role of a collaborator with the Turks. More recently, rumor had it, the disillusioned John had been involved in a shady—and unsuccessful—attempt to sell his claim to the imperial title to the king of France in return for a French castle and an annual pension. Yet, whatever his past behavior, by strict application of the custom of primogeniture, John's right to the Byzantine crown was better than Manuel's, and if Manuel was to be away for any length of time, John if not placated would surely attempt a coup.

It was the enthusiastic Marshal Boucicaut who finally effected the reconciliation between uncle and nephew. How better to assure John's loyalty, he reasoned, than to give him what he wanted all along—the crown? After all, *someone* would have to be designated as regent during Manuel's absence. The exiled John VII was summoned to Constantinople; his rank as co-emperor was recognized, and for as long as Manuel was gone, he would be regent.[7] Though unfortunately John VII would never completely abandon his habits of devious intrigue, he seems on the whole to have made a genuine effort to prove himself worthy of his uncle's trust during Manuel's long absence in the kingdoms of the West.

16

Journey to the Westlands

Late in 1399, Manuel left Constantinople and journeyed with his wife Helena and their little sons to his brother Theodore in the Morea. Helena and the children would remain there while he traveled on to the West. In the vast bulk of the emperor's literary output, we search long and hard for a few glimpses into his mind and heart, and we find one when he speaks of the difficulty of parting from his family. "Oh, how was I able to endure the separation?" he recalled later, in writing to his eldest son, the future John VIII.[1]

We could wish that Manuel had written more of his journey to the Westlands,[2] but the mundane hardships of travel were, in his opinion, hardly a worthy subject for the imperial pen. Apparently he was not one who enjoyed traveling for its own sake. "The route was troublesome," he commented briefly, "and the events along it were not particularly pleasant."[3] The exact course followed by the emperor and his retinue across Italy is uncertain at points, but we do know that at length he entered France, the homeland of Marshal Boucicaut, the land on which he pinned his highest hopes. Wherever he went, huge crowds turned out to see the Emperor of the East who had journeyed from afar, like one of the wise men of old. They were not disappointed. Manuel chose to dress in solid white, and with his long white hair and flowing beard, he was an awe-inspiring figure, every inch a sovereign. Perhaps the French did not realize white was the Byzantine mourning color. Just outside Paris, King Charles VI met the emperor and presented him with a magnificent white horse. The onlookers watched in admiration as Manuel displayed his physical agility; though he was fifty years old and looked considerably older, he transferred himself from his own horse to the one given him by the king without setting foot on the ground.[4] From there, Manuel rode in triumph into the French capital. It seemed an auspicious beginning for his visit to Charles' kingdom. Widely noticed, too, were Manuel's efforts to please his hosts. On his first meeting with the French sovereign, when King Charles lifted his hat, Manuel reciprocated, though to be hatless, even for a moment, was strictly contrary to Byzantine etiquette.

Weeks passed, and negotiations moved slowly, but Manuel was optimistic. He was having a pleasant time at the French court; feted and entertained as visiting royalty should be, surrounded by luxuries far surpassing the paste jewels and earthen tableware of Blachernai Palace, and with the threat of the Turks hundreds of miles away. There were hunting parties, trips to holy shrines, and a great deal of talk about how France intended to help Byzantium.

Then came the blow like a bolt from the blue: Charles VI, the young king, was dangerously ill; his mind had snapped. Rumors flew like wildfire. How had it happened? A few years earlier, the king, riding through a forest, had been frightened by a "wild man of the woods," and suffered a nervous collapse. Though for a while he seemed to have recovered, his illness had now returned. The King of France believed he was made of glass and was in terror that he would break. He was violent and contrite in turn; and obviously unable to rule. The French court became a hotbed of intrigue, and not one of the rival factions contending for the power behind the throne had time, much less financial aid, for the impoverished sovereign of Byzantium.

Manuel decided to travel on to England. He knew his history, and must have reflected on the fact that among his predecessors, none but the first Constantine had visited the fog-wrapped isle in the northern sea. He had probably heard, too, how the British claimed Constantinople's founder among their native sons. More important, however, was the present state of affairs. The new English king, Henry IV, was known to talk a great deal about forming a crusade against the Turks. Manuel spent Christmas 1400 with the English court at the Palace of Eltham, and once again his letters home took on an optimistic note.

Of how the English reacted to the Eastern sovereign in their midst we hear little. One chronicler, however, Adam of Usk, who mentions the emperor's visit, tells us a great deal in a few words: "I thought within myself, what a grievous thing it was that this great Christian prince from the farther East should perforce be driven by unbelievers to visit the islands of the West, to seek aid against them. My God! What dost thou, ancient glory of Rome? Shorn is the greatness of thine empire this day. . . ."[5]

It soon became obvious that however much Henry IV of England may have dreamed of crusades, his hold on his own crown was so insecure as to afford him little opportunity to aid the Byzantine sovereign. Realizing the futility of a prolonged visit in England, Manuel and his retinue went back to Paris, where they spent long months of waiting and listening to unfulfilled promises. King Charles was still insane, with occasional lucid periods, and it was mainly to the various nobles that Manuel now presented his pleas. The traveling emperor no longer seemed a celebrity to the French court; they saw him now only as a tiresome, long-winded old man who wanted money, a schismatic Greek whose religious beliefs, they felt, were the next thing to heresy, and who could not even speak the French tongue. Manuel, vastly bored, homesick, and discouraged, consoled himself with literary pursuits and composed in full rhetorical style a description of a tapestry that adorned the wall of his lodging in the Louvre.

When deliverance came, it was from an unexpected quarter. Out of Central Asia straight into the lands of the Ottomans poured the savage hosts of Timur the Tartar, fierce nomads bent upon looting more than actual conquest. The Ottomans mustered their forces against them, and in the ensuing battle, old Sultan Bayazid was taken prisoner. The Tartars, laden with plunder and captives, at length withdrew to the lands from which they came, but the Ottoman state they left behind them was a shambles—at least until Bayazid's heirs might restore some semblance of order.

The Turks' loss was Byzantium's gain; the sudden, devastating campaign of Timur would give the emperor and his people a much-needed breathing space. When Manuel received news of these developments, he knew it was time to go home.

In the spring of 1403 Manuel returned to his empire. He would reign twenty-two years longer, years through which, against all probability, he managed to preserve his empire's freedom. An astute politician, he played off the sons of the fallen Sultan Bayazid against each other and at length managed to come to terms with the victorious Mehmet I, who owed his throne to some extent to Manuel's support. The two sovereigns, if not real friends, were at least respectfully tolerant of each other. There seemed hope that the Byzantine state might continue this *modus vivendi* indefinitely, side by side with its Turkish neighbor. While Manuel never ceased to hope that the Christians of the West would eventually organize a crusade on Byzantium's behalf, he learned to walk cautiously in his dealings with the sultan. The Ottoman state recovered from the ravages of the Tartars with surprising rapidity, and if Byzantium were to survive until help should come from the West, it would be by the sultan's grace. Manuel possessed a measure of statesmanship equaled by only a few of the emperors before him. While he lived, Byzantium's continued existence was assured.

17

"Sweeter than All Sweet Things..."

Perhaps one of the most serious problems facing Manuel on his return from his Western journey was the question of what he should do about his nephew and co-emperor John VII. Though John had governed with surprising ability during Manuel's absence, the young emperor had shown himself to be entirely too pro-Turkish. His uncle, upon learning of some of his intrigues, was so angry that according to common gossip he proclaimed he never wanted to see him again. John was banished to the isle of Lemnos. Not many months later, however, when Manuel's wrath had cooled, a new settlement was effected and John VII was dispatched to Thessaloniki. There, for the rest of his life, he reigned as "Basileus of all Thessaly," and since he had no surviving sons of his own, at his death the territory reverted to Manuel's branch of the family.[1] In this way, the long-standing feud between the descendants of John V was settled at last, and it is to the credit of both Manuel and his nephew that the final compromise was effected peaceably.

Throughout his long reign whenever he could spare time from his administrative duties, Manuel continued to derive great pleasure from literary pursuits. "The ability to write," he once commented, "is clearly sweeter than all sweet things and brings the greater glory."[2]

Unfortunately, however, though he produced a great number of compositions, the rhetorical conventions of his time caused him to reveal little of himself in his works. One choice exception to his usually impersonal style comes in a letter to his friend, Demetrios Chrysoloras. Here the emperor tells how his heavy schedule of work often caused him to skip meals, and how it was sometimes nearly dawn before he was able to get to bed. Custom decreed that the palace servants should begin their house-cleaning duties at daybreak, and though Manuel complained about "the shouting of the servant crew, ringing through the house in which I would like to sleep," it apparently would not have occurred to him to alter their schedule. "These people are most annoying, buzzing about the doors," he commented, ". . .yet the unavoidability of their function prevents any hindering of the disturbance."

After a short rest, Manuel habitually greeted the persons who had come to the palace to present their grievances to the sovereign and to seek his judgment on various matters of dispute. It was a tiresome business, day after day, year after year, and Manuel's letter reveals how much he might have wished to avoid it. "It is impossible to evade . . . those whosoever are burdened with his particular problem: nay, there stands Latin, Persian [Turk], citizen, foreigner—even monk, no less—each demanding something else, and each shouting that he would be done injustice if he should not forthwith receive what he wants. . . . The best thing that could happen is something, anything, that would deliver me from these troublesome creatures each day."[3]

Manuel was weary. Though he was blessed with good health and unusual stamina for a man of his age, he was growing old and the lack of sufficient leisure for his literary studies vexed him, sometimes as he admitted, leaving him "practically in tears."[4] Still to those around him, he presented a gracious exterior. Deeply committed to his sovereign duties, he strove consistently for justice. Though there are hints that he occasionally displayed a burst of temper, he possessed, too, a redeeming sense of humor and a genuine kindness that won him the devotion of practically all who knew him well.

Some of the most vivid glimpses of Manuel's court and of Constantinople during his reign come from the account of a Spanish envoy, Ruy Gonzáles de Clavijo, who visited the Byzantine capital late in 1403.[5] When Clavijo called at Blachernai Palace, he was granted an audience with Manuel and Helena. Their three eldest sons were also present; John, the first-born, must have been small for his age, for Clavijo guessed he was about eight years old when actually he was almost eleven. Though the Spaniard gives no further description of the physical appearance of the imperial family, he does present graphic details concerning the throne room. Manuel was "seated on a raised dais, carpeted with small rugs, on one of which was spread a lion skin and at the back was a cushion of black stuff embroidered in gold."[6] The emperor and Clavijo talked, presumably with the aid of an interpreter, for some time. Later that day, when the envoy and his retinue returned to their lodgings in Pera, they were pleased to receive the gift of a stag, just slain by the emperor's huntsmen.

In the days that followed, Clavijo toured the city. Like most medieval travelers, he was particularly concerned to see the numerous holy relics contained in its churches. When Manuel promised him a glimpse of certain relics ordinarily kept under lock and key, Clavijo was delighted, but on the appointed day Manuel went hunting and left the key with Helena, who failed to send it for Clavijo's use. The disappointed Spanish envoy was still able to see the public sights; he gazed admiringly at the lovely mosaics in a number of the local churches, particularly Hagia Sophia, and visited the Hippodrome where he stared in wonder at the ancient obelisk of the Emperor Theodosius I and pondered over the hieroglyphic inscription upon it which none whom he asked could translate. Similar sightseeing trips occupied Clavijo for several days thereafter. Always his primary interest was holy relics, but he also took time to note the ruins of the notorious windowless tower of Anemas, dismantled by John V. Ultimately Manuel provided the key to the most venerable deposit of relics, and Clavijo was able to view these treasures to his heart's content.[7]

But as much as he found to praise in Constantinople—the emperor's graciousness towards him and the inspiring sight of the many relics—Clavijo's overall impression of the Byzantine capital is one of sad decay. "Though the circuit of the walls is . . . very great and the area spacious, the city is not throughout very densely populated. There are within its compass many hills and valleys where corn fields and orchards are found, and among the orchard lands there are hamlets and suburbs which are all included within the city limits," he reports.[8] Well might he have reflected that far more miraculous than the saints' bones and holy icons he beheld with such awe was the fact that the Empire of Byzantium still existed at all.

Among Manuel's endeavors to increase the security of his empire, none is more interesting than the project that he undertook in 1415 to fortify the Isthmus of Corinth and thus protect the entrance to the Morea.[9] By this time, Manuel's brother Theodore was dead, and the Despotate of the Morea had passed to Manuel's young son, who was called Theodore II. Composed of an assortment of territories in Southern Greece, the Morea was a detached piece of the empire, where in spite of the Byzantine emperor's *détente* with Sultan Mehmet I, there was always the danger of Turkish encroachment.

Manuel's plan for strengthening the Morea called for the rebuilding and fortification of the Hexamilion, the ancient wall across the isthmus built in the reign of the great Emperor Justinian I, almost a thousand years earlier.

Sultan Mehmet was aware of Manuel's plan, but apparently was not too concerned, believing it simply could not be done. The emperor believed otherwise, and set out from Constantinople determined to construct a wall that would stand forever.

Looking back later on the difficulties he encountered, Manuel commented that the stormy sea as he sailed to his destination should have warned him of the troubles that still lay ahead. The voyage was miserable with "thunderclaps echoing in our ears . . . and continuous bolts of lightning flashing in our eyes, together with furious rainstorms and snowstorms in some places." As waves rose over the decks, the emperor truly believed that his ship would go down, and when he finally reached land, he declared he went ashore still trembling. "To tell the whole story, the voyage was just the sort of thing to tear out our best hopes by the roots."[10]

When Manuel reached the Morea, there was more trouble waiting for him. The rebuilding of the Hexamilion—so called since it was approximately six miles long—would demand more funds than the imperial treasury could spare.

As Manuel observed, "there is . . . little wealth within our borders; . . . not so much as would strain the hand of him who carries it off."[11] The Moreotes would themselves simply have to contribute to the building project. Some did so willingly, agreeing with the emperor's optimistic predictions that the new fortifications would afford them more complete security than they had ever known. Opposition arose, however, from some of the local lords who saw this outburst of activity from the aged basileus as a direct threat to their own independence—and lawless conduct. Manuel, they felt, should have stayed in Constantinople; and they were definitely not going to help with the Hexamilion. The project began anyway, and Manuel, like the Biblical wallbuilder Nehemiah, faced the taunts and threats of the opposition as he endeavored to keep his men at work. In twenty-five days the work was completed; but the enemies of the enterprise continued to make so much trouble that eventually there was an open battle between them and the emperor's forces. Manuel was victorious; the defeated Moreote lords accepted, however reluctantly, the curbs he placed on their lawless behavior—and, presumably, contributed to the wall-building fund as well. Manuel could rest satisfied that the ordinary folk of the province could now tend their crops and pasture their animals without fear of enemy raids. He had done a great work; he was discouraged by the opposition, but his determination had triumphed in the end.

A few years later, when Manuel was in his seventies he suffered a stroke that left him a bedridden semi-invalid. Along with the physical damage came realization of the fact that his mind was not so clear as it used to be—and yet clear enough to be painfully aware of his growing incapacity and to realize that his son John VIII, whom he officially recognized as his co-emperor, must do the ruling for him. Manuel worried a great deal about John. Like most fathers, he was full of advice: continue to seek the friendship of the Westlands, but don't offend the Turks . . . don't do anything rash . . . above all, be faithful to our Orthodox faith. . . . John listened respectfully, made little comment, and proceeded to do exactly as he pleased.

"My son the basileus," Manuel remarked on one occasion to one of his close confidants, the future chronicler Sphrantzes, "is a fitting basileus, yet not so for the present time. For he sees and thinks on a grand scale, such as occasions warranted in the prosperity of our forefathers. But today . . . our troubles are crowding close upon us . . . and I fear lest from his schemes and endeavors there may come ruin for this house. . . ."[12]

But if Manuel worried about his son, he knew also that he must trust him, different as John's ways might be from his own. "Do as you wish," he said, "for I, my son, am old and near to death. The realm and all things pertaining to it, I have given to you, so do as you wish."[13] John proceeded to act on this advice and stirred up a complicated intrigue against the new Sultan Murad II, son of Mehmet I, who had succeeded to the Ottoman throne in 1421. The result was a Turkish siege of Constantinople that lasted throughout the whole of 1422. When Murad's forces were unable to penetrate the city's excellent fortifications, the Turks turned to the Morea, and broke through Manuel's Hexamilion. Peace terms when finally concluded recognized John VIII's vassalage to the sultan. The advantages that Manuel had gained in the years immediately following Timur's invasion were now irretrievably lost.

In 1425, realizing that the end was near, Manuel exchanged his imperial garb for the traditional robes of a monk and took the name of Brother Matthias. A few weeks after his seventy-fifth birthday, he died, in the summer of 1425.

No sovereign is ever universally esteemed, yet the Byzantines loved Manuel Palaiologos as few rulers have ever been loved. There was gentleness in him, but not weakness. We hear almost nothing in Manuel's reign of the cruel mutilations that were a standard part of Eastern justice; yet he had, perhaps (his troubles with the Moreote lords not withstanding), as few internal enemies as any emperor had possessed. It was as if people realized that Manuel was himself the living embodiment of the empire— old, venerable, bowed with the weight of a stormy past and an inevitable future. Now he was gone, and that future, for good or ill, lay in the hands of his sons.

18

The Renaissance Basileus

John VIII was at the same time a Renaissance prince and a Byzantine basileus. That he played both roles with considerable aplomb is reflected in his magnificent portrait frescoed on the wall of the Medici Chapel in Florence. Seated astride a splendid white horse, John Palaiologos is clad in a fashionable brocade tunic of green and gold; his dark face, beneath a mass of curly brown hair, is serenely aristocratic; his beard is short and neatly curled, more in the style of the Renaissance West than of Orthodox Greece. On his feet are the traditional red boots of the basileus and golden spurs; on his head, a crown adorned by a great many feathers and a few smallish jewels.

The fresco was not painted from life, but the artist Gozzoli undoubtedly had studied authentic likenesses of John and relied also on the verbal recollections of many who had seen him face to face. Consequently, one is tempted to wonder if this headdress really existed. If so, it must have been a low-budget crown—a great deal of magnificence for relatively little expense. John VIII never had much money, but he loved splendor and was determined to make the best of a bad situation. The empire he ruled consisted of little more than one city. Throughout his

long reign it hovered on the verge of collapse, but the
Emperor John would never think of abandoning the niceties that had surrounded his predecessors. "The emperor's
state is as splendid as ever," wrote one visitor to Constantinople at this time, "for nothing is omitted from the
ancient ceremonies, but, properly regarded, he is like a
bishop without a See."[1]

In many ways, John is a more elusive personality than
his father Manuel. Perhaps this is because he seemingly
inherited none of his father's love of writing and we have
no autobiographical glimpses of him. It is reported that he
very much enjoyed music, that he delighted in listening to
Castilian ballads sung to the accompaniment of a lute.[2]
Nonetheless, John was basically an outdoors man; the
artist Gozzoli did well to depict him on horseback, for John
had a passion for riding. Hunting was by far his favorite
pastime, and if we are to believe the complaints of some of
his courtiers, he devoted so much time to the sport as to
neglect state business. Be that as it may, the vigorous
physical exercise he had in the chase helped to make him
into an excellent soldier. During the latter years of his
father's reign, he obtained a great deal of military experience as commander of the imperial forces in the Morea.
There a seemingly endless struggle for power was being
waged between the Byzantines and certain Italian and
Spanish aristocratic families, descendants (literally or
figuratively) of the crusaders of 1204. In their little
principalities they still posed a formidable challenge to
Byzantine authority. In this turbulent world, separated from
Constantinople by many miles of Turkish-occupied territory, the Palaiologan princes maintained a precarious existence. It was a milieu in which intrigue flourished; in which
young men like John and his brothers might dream dreams of
grandeur and hope for a future in which Byzantium's
vanished power would be reborn.

Still while old Manuel lived, John usually attempted to
be a dutiful son. He seems, for instance, to have acquiesced

without protest when Manuel chose him a bride: a Russian princess, Anna of Moscow, aged eleven. John himself was twenty-two. The Russian chroniclers duly recorded Anna's journey to Constantinople to marry "Ivan Manuelovitch," and the young princess was installed in apartments of Blachernai Palace. John saw little of his child-bride, however, since he was absent on military campaigns in the Morea during most of their brief marriage. At fourteen, Anna died of the plague and John, we may suppose, did not grieve long for the little Russian who was almost a stranger to him.

Two years later, on to the scene came Sophia Monteferrata, Manuel's choice for John's second bride.[3] The selection of the Italian Sophia, a distant cousin of the Palaiologoi, was supposed to promote East-West good will, but as far as John was concerned, this objective failed miserably. One look at the young lady was enough to convince him he wanted nothing more to do with her. Poor Sophia was very large, larger, it would seem, than John. Her hands and arms were pretty, and she had spectacular curly reddish blonde hair, which when unfastened, reached to her feet. Having noted this, one had considered all of Sophia's good points, for her face was uncommonly homely.[4]

Early in 1421, John and Sophia were married, for to refuse her would be disobedience to Manuel and might also cause an international incident of grave proportions. But though he went through the ceremony, he did not have to live with her, John reasoned. The rejected princess was banished to a remote corner of Blachernai Palace, while John amused himself with casual mistresses and no doubt dreamed of the day when he would be able to rid himself of Sophia for good.

John was in his early thirties in 1425 when Manuel died and he became sole emperor. Sophia realized all too well the hopelessness of her position; it was only a matter of time, she knew, until John would seek to divorce her.

Rashly, the homely princess determined to act first. One day she set out from Blachernai Palace with a small group of Italian ladies and gentlemen attendants for an all-day outing. Before the day was over, they crossed to Pera, where a Genoese ship was waiting by prior arrangement to carry her back to her homeland. She took with her only one souvenir of her marriage: her crown, to prove that she had once been empress, if only for a little while.

Many Constantinopolitans had a warm spot in their hearts for poor ugly Sophia. There was great public outcry when they learned of her disappearance: "The Genoese have stolen our empress!" But the Emperor John was in no mood to try to bring her back; he was so delighted to be rid of her he could not afford to feel embarrassed over her flight. Sophia's subsequent entry into an Italian convent gave him freedom to seek a third bride, and this time at last, good fortune smiled upon him. On the advice of his envoy Bessarion, he chose a lady he had not yet met face to face but who in time turned out to be the great love of his life: his distant cousin, Maria Komnene of Trebizond.

The little state of Trebizond on the southern coast of the Black Sea boasted that its women were the greatest beauties in the world, and Maria Komnene certainly fitted the description. A few years after her marriage, in 1433, Bertrandon de La Brocquière, A Burgundian traveler with a ready pen, visited Constantinople. His memoirs provide a fascinating glimpse of the charming princess of Trebizond. He spied her first in Hagia Sophia, where the imperial family was watching a religious drama about the Hebrew children in the fiery furnace. Maria "seemed very handsome," La Brocquière noted, "but as I was at a distance, I wished to have a nearer view. And I was also desirous to see how she mounted her horse, for it was thus she had come to church. . . . " Burgundian ladies rode sidesaddle and La Brocquière could scarcely believe rumors that the Empress of Byzantium had not adopted this refinement.

The determined Burgundian tourist was destined to

have a long wait, however, for when Maria left the church, she went into a nearby house to dine and lingered there for some hours. La Brocquière had "to pass the whole day without eating and drinking," but as his narrative continues: "At last she appeared. A bench was brought forth and placed near her horse, which was superb and had a magnificent saddle. When she had mounted the bench, one of the old men [who accompanied her] took the long mantle she wore, passed to the opposite side of the horse, and held it in his hand extended as high as he could; during this she put her foot in the stirrup, and bestrode her horse like a man. When she was in her seat, the old man cast the mantle over her shoulders, after which one of those long hats with a point, so common in Greece, was given to her; at one of the ends it was ornamented with three golden plumes, and was very becoming."

La Brocquière also had time to notice Maria's ruby earrings and to observe the fact that she wore heavy cosmetics though "assuredly she had no need of it." "She looked young and fair and handsomer than when in church," he recalled in his memoirs, adding significantly, "I was so near that I was ordered to fall back, and consequently had a full view of her."[5]

If La Brocquière enjoyed this brush with Byzantine royalty, the Byzantine court also enjoyed him. The Emperor John was particularly eager to learn if there were any truth to the reports he had heard of a wonder-working warrior maiden who led the armies of France to incredible victories and yet, recently, had been taken prisoner by enemy forces. La Brocquière reported what he knew of Joan of Arc,[6] but although it was almost two years since her execution, he apparently had not yet learned of the final chapter in the Maid's career, so slow were communications between East and West.

During his weeks in Constantinople, La Brocquière attended several court functions, including the marriage of one of the Palaiologos cousins. He also toured the city, gazed with reverent delight at the numerous holy relics enshrined in the various churches, and like Clavijo a generation earlier, puzzled over the great stretches of open land within the city limits. These areas that had reverted to open country were sometimes farmed, sometimes left to lie as wasteland. The great walls of Constantinople simply encompassed an area too large for the diminished population.

One of La Brocquière's most vivid glimpses of the city's decay comes in his mention of the abandoned Hippodrome. No longer a center of public activities, the great stadium stood in ruins, and occasionally young nobles might be found there playing polo and similar games. One day, La Brocquière observed the emperor's brother Demetrios and a group of about twenty young horsemen enjoying a contest of skill they had learned from the Turks. "Each had a bow, and they galloped along the inclosure, throwing their hats before them, which, when they had passed, they shot at; and he who pierced his hat with an arrow, or was nearest to it, was esteemed most expert."[7] Demetrios, as time would prove, was not often occupied in such harmless pursuits.

From the memoirs of a Spanish traveler, Pero Tafur, come additional glimpses of Constantinople in the days of John VIII. Pero, a wealthy Castilian knight, came to the imperial city in 1437 to trace the reputed connection between his family and the Byzantine royal house, and in pursuit of this knowledge ingratiated himself with the emperor. John VIII's researchers (probably with the aid of considerable imagination) speedily turned up an impressive but vague family tree for Pero and the emperor proceeded thenceforth to call him "cousin." In the days that followed, the Castilian frequently accompanied the emperor and empress and their courtiers on hunting expeditions, while John (who no doubt believed the Byzantines could use all the help they could get) tried to persuade Pero to stay in Constantinople for good.[8]

Like La Brocquière, Pero was struck by the sad emptiness of the once great city. Blachernai Palace itself was, he reported, "now in such a state that both it and the city show well the evils which the people have suffered and still endure." The exterior of the palace was apparently impressive enough. At the entrance there was a large open loggia, with stone benches and tables; this area apparently adjoined the imperial archives where "books and ancient writings" were stored. Most of the palace, however, Pero reported, was in a sad state of deterioration: "the house is badly kept, except certain parts where the emperor, the empress, and attendants can live, although cramped for space."[9] While John insisted on full adherence to the niceties of court etiquette, Pero mentions incidentally that he was allowed not only to sit in the emperor's presence but "beside him," apparently on the same couch, an indication that Byzantine formality was still a long way from the rigid ceremonialism of the Baroque courts of Western Europe a few centuries later.

Pero's travels took him on from Constantinople to points further east, but later he returned for another visit to the Byzantine capital. The emperor was absent in Italy by this time, but the Spaniard enjoyed the hospitality of John's brother, the Despot Constantine, who conducted him personally on a tour of Hagia Sophia.[10] It is a disappointment in reading Pero's memoirs to find that he has so little to tell of Constantine, beyond the fact that he was a gracious and courteous host.

Of John's five younger brothers, Constantine, who eventually succeeded him as emperor, was apparently always the one whom John trusted most—perhaps the only one he could trust at all. According to the terms of the old Emperor Manuel's will, John, as the eldest son, inherited sovereignty over Constantinople and its immediate surroundings, while the younger sons were to divide among themselves the few remaining remnants of Byzantine territory not contiguous with the capital. Not one of them was really satisfied with what he received. Constantine, undoubtedly the best of the lot, occasionally tried to promote a spirit of cooperation among them, but the other four—Theodore, Andronikos (who died young), Demetrios, and Thomas—tended to cherish personal ambitions far more than brotherly loyalty. During John's reign, there was open war among them on more than one occasion, and continual intrigues into which even the high-minded Constantine was drawn.

As the years went by and Maria failed to present John with an heir, the matter of the imperial succession added fuel to the fire of the brothers' ambitions. By right of birth, Manuel's second son Theodore was heir presumptive, but if John were to have his way the succession would go to Constantine, (who remained unfailingly loyal), while Demetrios was determined, if possible, to get everything for himself. With his hands full of such family problems, it is no wonder that John began to lose the impetuous boldness that had made him dream in his youth of intrigues against the Ottoman Turks.

19

Ecumenical Efforts

John VIII clearly understood that the only realistic
option open to him was to recognize the sultan as his
overlord and to try to live in peace with him. And yet, if
the Christians of the West would come to Byzantium's
defense, it would be a different story. Gradually the old
specter of foreign aid, the elusive hope that had set his
father and grandfather before him on their futile journeys
to the Westlands, began to capture the imagination of the
Emperor John, and with it the prospect of reunion of
Orthodox and Catholic that had haunted the Byzantine
emperors for generations. John had himself been to Italy
and to Hungary once before. While his father Manuel was
still alive, in 1423, he had made a year's visit in the West:
in Venice, Milan, Mantua, and finally at the court of the
Holy Roman Emperor Sigismund, who was also King of
Hungary.[1]

Everywhere the reaction was the same: polite interest
in the plight of Byzantium but no help of substantial
proportions. If John had taken a lesson from this futile
experience, he would not have continued to hope so
greatly for eventual Western support. If he had taken a
warning from the experiences of some of his ancestors, he

would have dismissed any schemes for the union of the churches as impossible. And if he had heeded the more recent admonitions of his own father Manuel, he would have understood that to most Byzantines, submission to the pope would be betrayal of the faith. Do anything to win the favor of the Western powers, Manuel had counseled, only never accept their religion. Let them think we are interested in reunion, dangle the prospect before them, but never, never consummate it.

Perhaps he remembered Manuel's warnings, but above all John was irrepressibly optimistic and seems genuinely to have believed that he could succeed where emperors and popes for almost four hundred years had failed. The papacy itself was changing. The recent Great Schism of the West, during which two and then three rival popes had scandalized the Roman Catholic world for a generation, was officially ended. There was only one pope now, a stern, determined Venetian, Eugenius IV. He resided (at least part of the time) in Rome, where popes were supposed to live; not in Avignon, the charming little Frenchified state that had been the favorite home of many of his recent predecessors, and a bone of contention in the unholy prolonging of the schism. Pope Eugenius plainly meant business. Though he had no rival pope to deal with, he had his hands full of trouble from a group of independent-minded "Conciliar Fathers" who eventually assembled in Basle, Switzerland, to demand a democratizing of the Catholic Church that no medieval pope would have ever consented to. Pope Eugenius, like Emperor John, needed help. If the pope were able to effect a reunion of Eastern and Western Christendom, his prestige would soar mightily over the unruly fathers at the Council of Basle. John Palaiologos was clearly worth cultivating, thought the pope, particularly when he learned that the Basle fathers were also trying to negotiate with the Byzantine Emperor for reunion of the churches.

John, flattered by so much attention from the West, carefully weighed the alternatives, and decided to attend the council to be convoked by Pope Eugenius in Ferrara. Pope Eugenius promised to pay all the traveling expenses for the Byzantine delegation.

In the eyes of many of those going to the council, this was a boon too good not to be exploited to the fullest. A current witticism ran: How many quails can you eat for supper? Answer: If I'm paying, I'll take two; if the pope is paying, I'll have ten.[2]

It was late in November 1437 when the emperor left Constantinople for the grand adventure in ecumenicity. With him went the aged Patriarch Joseph, a host of Orthodox scholars and theologians, and his brother Demetrios (who was too dangerous to leave behind). A vast group of monks, courtiers, minor dignitaries, and servants accompanied the official delegation, bringing the total number of "Greeks" sailing for Italy to around seven hundred. Included among the baggage was John's gold-plated bedstead, an item that the emperor seemingly felt he could not do without.

Throughout the three months of their journey, stormy, rough weather was the almost constant companion of the Greek delegation. The Emperor John, who suffered gravely from arthritis, had to endure as well many bouts of seasickness, and once was so ill that he and his group took refuge on an uninhabited island for two days. The eighty-year-old patriarch, traveling aboard a different ship, was also a poor sailor; he insisted on going ashore every night if at all possible, even if he had to sleep in a tent. Without the numerous islands along the route, the Greeks were confident they would have never reached their destination.[3]

For some days the emperor avoided the sea altogether, when he decided to cross the Morea on horseback, and to spend the Christmas season visiting his brothers there.

He rejoined the voyage in January 1438, and after another month of wretched tossing at sea, the Greeks reached Venice, their point of debarkation.

Doge Francesco Foscari, determined to welcome John and the other Greeks in style, insisted that they remain aboard ship until the day following their arrival: the day designated for their official entry, complete with all the trimmings of Renaissance splendor.[4] The next morning when the festivities got under way, scarcely hindered by the misty, grey February weather, thousands of Venetians and visitors lined the banks of the city's canals to watch the pageantry of the emperor's arrival. Doge Foscari rode on the official state barge, the Bucentaur, which was magnificently decorated with vivid tapestries. Golden lions of St. Mark and Palaiologan eagles adorned the vessel's prow and the livery of the rowers. Trumpets and other instruments sounded; bells rang; hundreds of boats, official and unofficial, jammed the canals. Foscari and his son left their barge and boarded the emperor's ship, with an invitation for him to transfer himself to the Bucentaur for his ceremonial ride through the city. John refused. It seems altogether likely that the real reason for this diplomatic snub was the reluctance of the severely crippled emperor to walk at all with the eyes of the public upon him, as he would have to do in transferring from one vessel to another. John, however, never mentioned his physical handicap. Ever a stickler for etiquette, he pointed out that it would be unseemly for him to debark from a vessel furnished by a foreign power.[5] Foscari cannot have been pleased by the emperor's determination to have his own way, but he welcomed John most warmly, urged him to look upon Venice as his own city and to stay as long as he wanted. A few days after their arrival, both the emperor and the patriarch became ill and the Byzantine party of necessity was obliged to stay longer than they might have done otherwise. The Venetian government, which had planned to entertain them free for only about ten to twelve days, grew gravely concerned as the Greeks seemed likely to stay indefinitely.

It was about a month before they resumed their journey, by river boat up the Po, then to Ferrara where they would eventually confront Pope Eugenius in the full solemnity of the ecumenical council. As usual on such splendid occasions, John and his delegation were received in grand style outside Ferrara. Though the pope was nowhere in evidence, a group of cardinals and the Marquis of Ferrara were there to welcome the Orthodox visitors. John rode into the city on a black horse, while a team of canopy bearers marched on either side with a protective cover shielding the emperor from the rain. Before him went a riderless white horse, with a saddle cloth adorned with golden Palaiologos eagles.[6]

When John reached the city, the pope rose to greet him and gave him a brotherly embrace. They talked only briefly, but hopes were high for the success of the great enterprise. Many difficulties lay ahead, among them the inevitable problems of protocol: would Patriarch Joseph agree to kiss the pope's foot? (As it turned out, he would not.) But a spirit of compromise was in the air. The pope met the patriarch in private, and they kissed each other on the cheek as equals, if only for the moment.

From the outset, the Emperor John was convinced that the great meeting of East and West in Ferrara would attract delegations from practically all the courts in Europe, and urged postponement of the formal opening of the council for four months until they should arrive. The weeks passed; the visiting sovereign was installed comfortably in a palatial residence six miles outside Ferrara. In his rural retreat, John planned to have ample time for hunting while waiting for the council to begin. In the weeks that followed, the Marquis of Ferrara grew gravely concerned that John and the Greeks were depopulating his game; while some of the delegates, who were lodged in the city, complained that there was never any chance to get to see the emperor.[7]

John was usually in a good humor when occupied with the chase; he delighted in taking a large crowd with him, including attendants of relatively low status for whom an outing with the emperor was a rare privilege.[8] On the other hand, when Pope Eugenius presented him with a number of fine horses, John found none of them to his liking and purchased one that suited him better—a magnificent steed imported from Russia.

In spite of a few disquieting rumors of plague inside Ferrara, the summer passed most pleasantly, and with relatively little theology. It was about this time that Pero Tafur, now returning to Spain after extensive travels in the East, stopped in Ferrara to visit his "cousin" John and to bring him letters from the Empress Maria and the Despot Constantine. As might be expected, John was delighted to see Pero and begged him to stay indefinitely. The Byzantine emperor was not happy, however, that Pero had shaved off his beard. To shave was "a great wrong," John told him, for a beard "is the greatest honor and dignity belonging to man." Pero argued that Castilians held a different view; that in Spain a beard was not worn "except in cases of some serious injury" and that on returning to his own country he must follow native custom.[9]

Pero remained in Ferrara for some days, frequently dining at the emperor's table and accompanying him at least once on an official visit to the pope. Preliminary discussions on reunion—particularly on the vexed question of purgatory—were under way; but still no delegations had arrived from the princes of Western Europe.

As the weeks turned into months, it became increasingly obvious that no such emissaries would likely ever come. Pope Eugenius, who was paying the expenses of the visiting Greeks out of money he had borrowed himself, was growing more and more nervous, and further behind with his payments. There was no logical reason to postpone the official opening of the council any longer. A few of the Greeks had even gone home, discouraged by the long delay.

By the autumn of 1438, even the emperor seemed eager to get proceedings under way. There was, however, as John pointed out, the matter of his ceremonial entry into the council chamber: when the official opening day, October 8, 1438, came, John arrived on horseback. He intended to follow an old Byzantine custom and ride his horse straight to his throne. No indeed, the pope's attendants responded; no horses would be allowed inside the council hall. Well, John countered, they certainly didn't expect him to walk the whole length of the hall on foot, with hundreds of curious spectators watching his every step: it simply was not done that way in Constantinople. They would have to find a way to slip him in and get him seated without attracting attention. Since many a Byzantine emperor in centuries past had walked in many a procession, John's stubbornness was no doubt actually the result of his genuine difficulty in walking.

Fortunately there was a back entry, but it led through a room where the Patriarch Joseph and a great number of Orthodox monks were waiting for proceedings to begin. John sent an attendant, then brother Demetrios, then Demetrios again with a chamberlain to order Joseph and company to clear out of the room, but each time the patriarch refused (a revealing insight into the limits of the emperor's authority). Finally John was assisted—practically carried— through the back passage, with a throng of his own people watching, a situation almost as bad as being subjected to the prying eyes of the Latins.

Certainly, the emperor declared, he was not going to go through *that* again. There would simply have to be a way found for him to make a dignified entry even if it meant breaking through the wall behind his throne to construct a passage.[10]

The official date for the second session of the council was postponed for five days while the required renovation of the building got under way. Thereafter, John was carried through the rear halls of the council building and through the newly constructed back door near his throne. Here he was closely surrounded by a solid block of attendants, so the crowd could not see him until he was seated in all his splendor.

It was almost a year since the Greeks had left Byzantium, and now at last they were about to meet their Latin opponents in formal religious debate. Discussion in the weeks that followed centered around the addition of the word *filioque* to the Latin creed and the underlying differences between Greeks and Latins conveyed by this highly charged word. It is difficult to grasp the intense seriousness that the issue held for both sides: does the Holy Spirit proceed from God the Father alone, as the Byzantines maintained, or as the Latins believed, from the Father *and from the Son* (Latin, *filioque*)? At the end of two months the delegations were no closer to agreement than they had been at their first meeting. Meanwhile, the city of Ferrara reported a marked rise in the number of plague victims, and Pope Eugenius was falling further and further behind in his subsidies to the Greek delegation.

At this critical point, the Republic of Florence, no doubt at the prompting of its chief citizen, Cosimo de'Medici, offered a solution: let the council move to Florence, where there was no danger of plague and where the Florentine government would extend liberal credit to Pope Eugenius for maintenance of the Greeks. This proposal was acceptable to everyone, and in February 1439, the pope with his delegation, and John VIII, Patriarch Joseph, and their seven hundred Greeks all moved to Florence.

Thus it was that in later years, Gozzoli would paint

the famous fresco in the Medici Chapel commemorating the sojourn of these distinguished visitors in their city. So it was also that while John was still present in Florence, the artist Pisanello cast a bronze medal bearing the emperor's profile; a lifelike effigy that makes no attempt to conceal the sharply aquiline curve of his nose, and still conveys fully the sense of dignity that was so much a part of his being.[11] John's curly hair is styled in short, neat ringlets and in place of a crown he wears a tall pointed "Greek hat" with an upturned brim. One is reminded of La Brocquière's description of the Empress Maria's "Greek hat"; the same basic style was highly fashionable for both men and women at that time. Around the edge of the medal is inscribed: "John Palaiologos, Basileus and Autokrator of the Romans," and though we know how empty these titles were by his time, one feels that here was a man who bore them proudly.

But if John was sovereign of a dying state, he had brought his Greeks into a land overflowing with new ideas and new reverence for old ideas. The cultural Renaissance was much in the air in fifteenth-century Florence. To the humanist scholars of the city, the arrival of hundreds of Greeks who spoke the language of Plato as their native tongue was an event of first-rate importance. Some of John's entourage would never go home again: why return to a decaying empire when there were lucrative positions to be had in Italy as teachers of Greek language and literature? Thus however small the permanent results of the ecumenical council may have been theologically, the influx of the Byzantines into Florence is one of the major steps in the revival of Greek studies in Renaissance Europe.

Meanwhile the discussions of the council continued to drag on. It was no secret that the emperor wanted unification of the churches, but he allowed considerable freedom of speech to those of his delegation who did not share his viewpoint. Often the emperor and the Greek theologians held their conferences in the room of the aged Patriarch Joseph, whose strength was failing fast, but who still retained a lively interest in the proceedings.

Throughout the long months of the council, the Emperor John, too, was often unwell, though he hated to admit it. "He was always ill and always insisting that he was well," one member of the delegation recalled later. On at least one occasion, however, John felt too weak to rise from his bed, and called the delegates to meet in his room. "He was so ill that he could not lift his head from his pillow, and could say only: 'I am ill and I don't know if I can manage to express what I want to say.' "[12]

John was not a man of superabundant patience, but all in all he managed rather well through the trying months of prolonged discussion in Florence. Then, at last, the Greeks and Latins arrived at a compromise which seemed at the time a master stroke of theological diplomacy: the Latin *filioque* clause with its doctrine of procession of the Holy Spirit from the Father *and from the Son* was deemed to mean the same as the procession of the Holy Spirit from the Father *through* the Son, a position the Greeks readily accepted. A basis for true reunion now existed, and the old Patriarch Joseph joyfully ratified the arrangement. A few days later he died. Having muddled his prepositions, what else could he decently do? remarked a Greek delegate who did not share the general enthusiasm for reunion.[13]

Events nonetheless moved swiftly in the weeks that followed. The official reunion of the churches, so long an elusive dream, seemed to have turned into a reality at last. John Palaiologos did not force the Orthodox delegates to sign the decree of union; most of them did so, however, though a few, including the treacherous Despot Demetrios, slipped away in disgust and returned early to Constantinople. John scarcely gave a thought to these dissenters; he was far too engrossed with the dreams of substantial foreign aid Byzantium would soon be receiving from the West if all went well.

Unfortunately, John had failed to account for one of the most important factors of all: the voice of his people. As rumors of the Council of Florence drifted back to Constantinople, the news of the reunion evoked heated protests. The Emperor John and his unionizers were sailing back to a city torn by religious upheaval.

It was early in February 1440 when John returned to his capital. Intense gloom hung over the city. The people had no welcome for their basileus; they felt he had betrayed them, trafficking with the Latins of the West—who were worse than the Turks. As John re-entered his own palace, the gloom deepened. Something was clearly wrong, something that had nothing to do with the Council of Florence. The Empress Maria was not there to greet her husband. John looked at his brother Constantine, and Constantine, usually so forthright, averted his gaze. At length it was the old Empress Mother Helena who broke the news:[14] Maria was dead; she had died of the plague just six weeks before, on John's own birthday, December 17.

The emperor's grief for his beloved Maria knew no bounds. For weeks he was inconsolable. The implementation of church union, even the day to day business of government fell neglected as he gave himself to mourning for his lost love. And then, when at last he began to come out of it, his mind turned to hunting.[15] In the sport he had always enjoyed there was release for the emotional tensions that continued their hold upon him.

Meanwhile, the people of the city murmured louder and louder. There were riots in churches when the attempt was made to introduce *filioque* in the creed or to invoke God's blessing upon Pope Eugenius. The union of the churches might exist on parchment, but obviously it could never be planted in the hearts of the Byzantines. John Palaiologos was a broken man: he could scarcely bear to think of the Council of Florence, much less try to implement the decisions made there.

Rumors of many sorts began to circulate. There were

always some Byzantines with such a deep sense of loyalty to the basileus, whoever he might be, that they felt obliged to concoct explanations for his behavior, past and present. It was this attitude that gave rise to tales of the Emperor John's remorse. According to this trend of thought, he was deeply ashamed that he had submitted to the Pope, and through his inaction was trying to undo what he had done in Florence. It is an interesting theory, but historically unsound. John Palaiologos, as long as he lived, remained personally committed to the union of Orthodox and Catholic. But he had grown weary of controversy; he knew he lacked the strength to make the union acceptable to his people. It was a problem which he would pass on unsolved to his successor Constantine, and as time would prove, Constantine with all his great tact and patience could not solve it either.

John lived on until 1448. These were hard years, years in which he witnessed the ever-increasing power of the Turks and the devastating defeat of the Western volunteers who joined with the forces of Christian Hungary in an attempt to reverse the tide. John remained neutral in these struggles. With the Ottoman Sultan as his overlord, he had little choice; but unquestionably he pinned his hopes on the Catholic Christians of the West. If only the fortunes of war had gone the other way, John's activities at Florence would have been vindicated, and his little empire would have been assured of a new lease on life.

Alas, it was not to be; for Byzantium and for John Palaiologos, time was running out. The end came for the Emperor John on the last day of October 1448. Because of his commitment to the union, the Orthodox Church refused him the funeral rites customary for a deceased emperor. He was buried quietly at Constantinople's Monastery of the Pantokrator, in the same grave with his Empress Maria.[16]

Meanwhile, John's crafty brother Demetrios moved swiftly in an attempt to seize the throne, but his plan was forestalled by his mother, the aged Empress Helena Dragases, who hurriedly sent word to Constantine, the right-ful heir, in the Morea. By the terms of John's will and by his own right as the oldest surviving son of Manuel, Constantine was indisputably emperor. To him would belong the glory and the tragedy of Byzantium's last days.

20

Constantine the Last

When Manuel Palaiologos and Helena chose to call their
fourth son "Constantine," they probably gave little thought
to the prophecy current for some centuries that the last
emperor of Byzantium would bear the same name as the first
one. "Constantine" was a good name, Manuel and Helena
believed; for one thing, it was the name of Helena's father.
And what if the imperial family had superstitiously tended
to avoid it in recent generations? There were no fewer than
ten Constantines among the emperors of earlier centuries,[1]
including the founder himself, Constantine the Great. Even
the name of the city, "Constantinople," was a reflection of the
name of Constantine. It was thus, Manuel must have
reasoned, a name that any Byzantine could be proud of.
Without further ado, the child was christened Constantine
Dragases Palaiologos. Anyone with superstitious qualms
about the matter could recall that, after all, a boy with so
many older brothers stood almost no chance of inheriting the
throne.

We know little of Prince Constantine's childhood. He
cannot have been close to his eldest brother, the future
John VIII, who was twelve years older than he; though in
later years, when the age difference mattered less, there

would be a strong bond of loyalty between them. Apparently far closer even than the brothers who were nearer his own age was Constantine's childhood friend, George Sphrantzes.[2] George's grandfather was Prince Constantine's tutor, and the two boys took their lessons together, studied, played, and grew up together. While destiny had decreed that Constantine would be Byzantium's last emperor, George Sphrantzes was to become a chronicler of the empire's last years. It is from him that some of our important knowledge of Byzantium's last days is derived.[3]

It would be worth a great deal had the Emperor Manuel, in all his voluminous writing, had more to say about his personal feelings for his own children, but unfortunately this is not the case. Still there are clues that suggest that Manuel was proud of his son Constantine. Though he never possessed his father's scholarly inclinations, Constantine was a young man of intelligence and ability. Even in his teens, his father frequently entrusted him with administrative responsibilities, in preference at times to his older brothers. On one occasion, when John was away and Manuel too old and ill to rule, the eighteen-year-old Constantine actually served as regent.[4]

Still, young Constantine harbored no dreams of the throne; he was much too far down in the line of succession. When Manuel died, he willed to this fourth son the town of Selymbria, some forty miles west of Constantinople. It was not much of an inheritance, but it was the best Manuel could do; one cannot be lavish when one has six sons and a very small empire.

Constantine did not remain in Selymbria. Not long after his brother John VIII became sole emperor, he departed for the Morea—summoned there by his brother, the Despot Theodore II.

Theodore, who was moody, unpredictable, and subject to recurrent bouts of depression, had just announced his intention of becoming a monk. The despotate, he promised, he would turn over to Constantine. Then when Constan-

tine arrived along with John VIII and Sphrantzes, Theodore declared he had changed his mind: he was not going to
enter a cloister after all.[5]

Constantine, disappointed in his hopes of obtaining a
larger appanage, decided to remain in Morea anyway, and
in the next few years, the Palaiologos brothers launched a
brilliant offensive against some of the "Frankish" (Italian
and Spanish) lords who held various bits of the surround-
ing area. Constantine was a skilled militarist, but he was
not one to enjoy fighting simply for its own sake. He was
an idealistic young man, who had great dreams for the
rebuilding of the Byzantine state. To him the campaign for
the consolidation of the Morea was a fight for Greek
independence from foreign domination. At first, his undertakings were crowned with repeated successes, including
restoration of his father Manuel's wall, the Hexamilion.
Constantine was an excellent soldier, physically brave and
intensely patriotic. Even more important, he was a good
man; patient, kind, endowed with great integrity. His
troops, the members of his household, his servants, his
close friends looked upon him with profound respect and
admiration. To many of the Greek people, young Constantine Palaiologos seemed a leader cast in the mold of the
heroes of classical antiquity.

It is ironic that while the sources tell us so much about
Constantine's personality, we have only vague descrip-
tions of his physical appearance. No authentic portrait of him from his own lifetime has survived. Reportedly, he was tall and slender, and probably dark of com-
plexion like his brother John. There is one portrait
sketched some years after his death that, although styl-
ized, might claim to be a reasonable likeness; Constantine's hair and beard are dark; his beard is short and neatly
rounded, in contrast to the long, flowing style affected by
some of his ancestors.[6] As he grew older, we may well
imagine that the lines of his face reflected some hint of the
cares that continually pressed upon him, for Constantine

Palaiologos was destined for a life filled with sorrow and disappointments.

Constantine was twenty-three when he married Magdalena-Theodora Tocco, an aristocratic young lady from a powerful family. The Toccos, though Italian, were thoroughly Byzantinized and became allies of Constantine in his struggle to oust the "Frankish" lords of the Morea. The wedding was celebrated at a military camp outside of the city of Patras, then under siege by Constantine's forces. Magdalena, who brought with her a handsome dowry, was an eminently suitable bride. Yet within little over a year after their marriage, she died in childbirth along with her newborn infant.[7]

Constantine waited until he was well in his thirties before he remarried. It was Sphrantzes who found him a second wife, Catarina (or Aikaterini) Gattilusi, a cousin of the Palaiologoi, from the Greco-Italian aristocracy of the Morea. The Gattilusi were the lords of the island of Lesbos, and it was there at one of her family's strongholds that Constantine spent his brief honeymoon with Catarina in the summer of 1441. Military duties soon called him away, and it was about a year before he returned for his bride. They had sailed only as far as Lemnos when they were attacked by the Turks. Constantine and Catarina took refuge in a fortified castle on Lemnos, where they were besieged by the enemy for twenty-seven days. Though they endured the siege, and were finally able to move on to Palaiokastro, Catarina's health was failing, because of the strain and stress of the long days of the blockade. Before the summer was over, she was dead.[8]

According to the laws of Greek Orthodoxy, Constantine had now had his two chances at matrimony. If he should ever seek to marry a third time, it could only be with a special dispensation from the church. In the years that followed, he gave the matter much consideration, but as it turned out, he remained a widower the rest of his life.

From the first of his wives, Magdalena, Constantine

inherited extensive land holdings in the Morea and there he continued to spend most of his time. This greatly irritated his older brother, the Despot Theodore, who resented Constantine's popularity and resented even more, as the years went by, the fact that John VIII was obviously inclined to designate Constantine as his heir. At one point, Theodore and Constantine actually went to war against each other. This unhappy state was finally resolved when Theodore pressured his brother into a territorial exchange which he believed would be most advantageous to himself: Constantine gave him Selymbria and he gave Constantine his rights to the Morea.[9] In Selymbria, so close to Constantinople, Theodore believed he would be better able to lay first claim to the throne of their brother John. Constantine acquiesced; his roots were in the Morea now, and if Selymbria had its advantages, peace among his brothers was worth more to him than personal ambition.

As Despot of the Morea, Constantine continued the struggle for Greek unification and independence. In 1444, his forces swept out of the Peloponnese on a large-scale invasion of northern Greece. The Italian duke of Athens temporarily accepted Constantine's overlordship but secretly called for aid from the Sultan Murad II. As Constantine's forces soon discovered, it was one thing to battle the petty Latin lords in their tiny Greek principalities, but quite another to take on the mightiest military power in the Eastern world: the Ottoman Turks. Although Constantine and his men fought with great determination, they were pushed back into the Morea. The Turks, moreover, followed the retreating Byzantines in hot pursuit, breaking through the Hexamilion and spreading devastation in their path. Thousands of Greeks were slain, and Constantine their despot was compelled to pay heavy tribute. It was a stunning blow, the end of the dream that he had pursued most of his life.

In the next few years, he spent much of his time in the Palace of the Despots of Mistra, a lonely man filled with memories of a great enterprise that had failed. Among his people there were many who had turned against him, who blamed him senselessly for the devastating defeat of their hopes, who whispered superstitiously that he was born under an unlucky star. His future was most uncertain. True, his brother John continued to indicate that he would succeed him on the imperial throne, but a great deal depended on whether, when the time came, Theodore, now Despot of Selymbria, should press his claim to the succession.

As it turned out, Theodore died of the plague a few months before John, and since Andronikos, the third brother, had been dead for many years, Constantine was unquestionably the rightful heir. The news of John VIII's death reached Mistra late in 1448. In early January 1449, the new Emperor Constantine XI proceeded to have himself consecrated basileus by the rites of the ancient coronation ceremony.[10] He defied convention, however, in having the service performed in a small church in Mistra, where a cracked stone paving square with the Palaiologos eagle carved upon it still marks the spot on which he stood for this occasion. Because he did not choose to be crowned in Constantinople, some sources imply that the rite lacked the validity of a proper coronation. Thus the historian Doukas, writing not long after Constantine's death, refused to consider him a true emperor. While such objections are meaningless, the fact that he was willing to forego the celebration of the ancient rite in Hagia Sophia indicates a great deal about Constantine XI. He believed firmly in the union of the Churches, as proclaimed by John VIII at Florence, yet he knew that the majority of his subjects did not. Public celebration in Constantinople of such an important rite as the coronation would surely give rise to a renewal of the controversy over the union. Constantine did not want upheaval.

Bitter winter weather delayed Constantine's arrival in his capital until more than four months after his brother

John's death. In the meantime, Helena Dragases held the throne for her absent son and frustrated the intrigues of Demetrios, who sought to claim it for himself.

In the early spring of 1449, the new emperor at last sailed to his capital, with a small fleet borrowed from the Genoese. Already there were some who were reflecting ominously on the fact that his name was "Constantine" and recalling the dread prophecy that Constantinople would fall when an emperor reigned who bore the founder's name. And to make matters worse, he was, like the founder, Constantine the son of Helena.[11] Constantine XI had no use for such superstitions. Perhaps he was worried, and in times to come he must have thought about the matter many times, but he was proud of his name and certainly did not intend to change it. In 1449, worry about the immediate fall of Constantinople appeared rather pointless; for years, John VIII had lived in relative peace with the Sultan Murad II, and there seemed no reason why Constantine might not do the same. Far greater causes for the new emperor's immediate concern were his quarrelsome brothers, Demetrios and Thomas, and his own lack of a wife. He set out at once to find solutions to these difficulties.

Not long after Constantine's arrival in the capital, the Empress-mother Helena presided over a ceremony in which Demetrios and Thomas publicly swore loyalty to their new emperor.[12] Constantine responded by dividing between them all his former possessions in the Morea, and the two co-despots departed soon thereafter for their new territory. The years that followed witnessed them more often than not at odds with each other, and when Constantine needed them, neither was able—or willing—to come to his aid.

For a little while, however, it seemed that Helena Dragases' peace-making efforts had succeeded. It was but one example of how the aged Helena, who long ago had taken the vows of a nun but who continued to live in

Blachernai Palace, was determined to do all in her power
to help Constantine her son. In spite of her religious vows,
Helena remained much a mother still. Apparently she
adored Constantine—him who far more than any of his
brothers reflected the gentle strength of his father Manuel.
And because she loved him, she worried a great deal about
him. She was full of advice on such diverse matters as the
union of the churches (which she opposed) and his own
quest for a suitable bride. Constantine, for his part, in
spite of the long years in which he had seen his mother
only rarely, now found her a close confidante. Helena died
in 1450, and there is some hint of Constantine's desolation
in a letter purportedly written by him not long thereafter
to his friend George Sphrantzes, who was absent on a
diplomatic mission to find Constantine a wife: "Since you
have gone abroad my mother has died. . . . There is no one
here with whom I can hold counsel; everyone looks solely
after his own private interests. Everyone of them belongs to
one party or another, and would betray to others [what-
ever] I might confide to him."[13]

Helena had urged Constantine to select a wife from an
Orthodox rather than a Latin country, for such a choice
would be more pleasing to his subjects. Realizing the
wisdom of this advice, Constantine sent Sphrantzes on his
quest to Trebizond and Russian Georgia.[14] While the
emperor's friend was away on this mission, an event of
greatest significance occurred: old Sultan Murad died and
was succeeded by his son Mehmet II, aged nineteen. The
Byzantines had lived in comparative peace with the Turks
for so many years now, there seemed little cause to worry
that the new young sultan would upset things.

From Constantine's point of view, infinitely more
interesting at the time was the fact that Mara Brankovitz,
a charming Serbian lady who had been—against her will—
a member of Sultan Murad's harem, was now free. Mara
was Constantine's distant cousin, and like him in the
midforties.[15] Her father, the aged George Brankovitz of

Serbia, was the richest Christian prince in the Balkans. The new sultan, moreover, considered Mara his "beloved stepmother" and she was reputed to have great influence with him. In view of these assets, Mara Brankovitz seemed an extremely suitable wife for the Emperor of Byzantium, and Constantine after some hesitation sent his proposal.[16] To his surprise and dismay, Mara refused him. She had taken a vow, she said, that if she ever escaped the harem, she would remain celibate forever after and devote her life to works of Christian charity. Her old father George, who was prepared to grant her a substantial dowry, was horrified: the idea that any woman should forego the chance to be Empress of Byzantium! Mara's refusal indeed may have altered the course of history: had she married Constantine, perhaps she could have convinced her stepson Mehmet to leave Constantinople in peace.

But since Mara refused, Constantine decided to continue negotiations for the hand of the princess of Georgia. The young lady accepted, and some months later was preparing to sail, when news from Constantinople convinced her it was too late.

21

The Siege

It was the new Sultan Mehmet II who so profoundly altered Constantinople's fortunes. The young man, as it turned out, was obsessed with the idea of conquering the Byzantine capital. He was known on occasion to sit up all night drawing diagrams of the city, planning possible attacks. *Blessed is he who shall conquer Constantinople,* the Prophet Muhammad had promised eight centuries ago. How many times in those centuries had the prophet's followers tried and failed to fulfill this objective! An ardent student of history, Mehmet realized the vast difficulty of taking a stronghold so well fortified and strategically located. Every detail of the city's defenses he studied at length. The magnificent harbor of the Golden Horn, he knew was still guarded by the famous boom that had kept out enemy fleets on many previous occasions. One end of this huge chain was fastened down in Pera, the Genoese outpost across the harbor from Constantinople. Mehmet did not want to risk war with the powerful Republic of Genoa. Best to leave the boom alone and concentrate on planning an assault on Constantinople by land. Mehmet was fully informed of the intricacies of the triple walls on the landward side of the city and of the gigantic foss or trench beyond the outermost wall. The foss was sixty feet wide and about half as deep, a veritable moat without water in it.[1] Mehmet seemed to take a positive delight in the logistical difficulties that Constantinople's conquest presented; so much the greater would be the glory of the city's conqueror.

Unfortunately, the rumors of Mehmet's obsessive preoccupation with the conquest of Constantinople were not taken seriously by the advisors of Constantine XI. The sultan was a young man, and in the first months of his reign faced considerable opposition from rebellious elements within his own army. It would be an ideal time, so the emperor and his advisors believed, to approach Mehmet on a touchy subject: the question of Byzantium's continued maintenance of the Turkish Prince Orkhan, a pretender to the sultan's throne. Orkhan had lived in Constantinople for years, and the old Sultan Murad, grateful to have this potentially dangerous rival safely under the protective custody of the Byzantine emperor, sent a sizable annual subsidy for his continued retention. Constantine, faced with a sadly depleted treasury, felt he might demand of Mehmet an increase in this subsidy payment; if the sultan refused, the Byzantines would let Orkhan loose to claim Mehmet's throne.[2]

The demand was a serious mistake. Though Mehmet replied coolly that he would think it over, the whole incident merely added fuel to his burning desire to conquer Constantinople. As soon as he had suppressed the rebellious elements in his own army, he turned to the first step in his plan for the final destruction of the Byzantine Empire. In the spring of 1452, Turkish workmen suddenly appeared in Byzantine territory at a spot on the Bosphoros coast just north of Constantinople. There they started construction of a fortress. The purpose was all too obvious. The new fortification, together with an already existing Turkish fort just across the Bosphoros, would patrol all traffic in and out of the Black Sea. Constantinople was about to be cut off from any contact with the area from which most of the city's grain supply came.

When Constantine sent ambassadors to protest on at least two separate occasions, the sultan refused to answer them satisfactorily.[3] Meanwhile the building of the fortress continued, and Constantine sent additional envoys. This time, Mehmet no longer ignored them; he had them thrown into prison and beheaded. It was clear that the building of the fortress, Rumeli-Hisar as the Turks called it, was symptomatic of far worse provocations to come. The Emperor Constantine turned his full attention to preparing for the siege that was sure to come. He ordered inspection of the city walls and repairs wherever needed; he collected food supplies. His friend Sphrantzes was assigned the task of conducting a census of able-bodied fighting men in the city. The findings were so depressing that Constantine ordered the information kept secret: the total number of prospective defenders was somewhat less than seven thousand men.[4] The Sultan Mehmet, it was reported, had almost eighty thousand men under his command, more than the entire population of Constantinople.

If the Byzantine capital were to survive, there would simply have to be assistance from the West. Through all of 1452, imperial envoys traveled in Italy appealing for aid.[5] The response was not enthusiastic. Most of the Italian states did not believe Constantinople would really fall; there had been such alarms before and they had proved groundless. The religious question, too, was uppermost in many minds.

Pope Nicholas V promised aid only if Constantine should succeed in implementing the Union of the Churches proclaimed at Florence some years earlier and disdained by most Byzantines ever since. "We have not the least doubt," wrote the pope to Constantine, "that John Palaiologos, your brother and predecessor on the throne . . . could, had he so wished, have brought this business to a happy conclusion, but, because he was too intent on adjusting it to his temporal situation, he was taken from your midst."[6]

This unkind and undiplomatic pronouncement—a surprising revelation of stubbornness in the usually mild-mannered Pope Nicholas—must have seemed like a slap in the face to Constantine XI. Still the emperor genuinely wanted the union, and with the pope's position so unequivocally stated, he would do all in his power to accomplish it. In Constantinople, the emperor's unionizing tendencies met with vast opposition. Looking back across the centuries and recalling his incomparable heroism in the empire's last days, it is hard to realize that many of his own subjects hated him cordially while he lived and considered him a traitor to Orthodoxy. "Better the sultan's turban than the cardinal's hat"[7]—this slogan attributed to the Admiral Lukas Notaras sums up the attitude of those who firmly resisted Constantine's efforts to bring Orthodox and Catholic together as one Christian faith. "Unionist" worship services were boycotted by the majority of the city's inhabitants. Constantine could do nothing more, short of resorting to force, and because he was a Byzantine himself and understood fully the strange, tragic stubbornness of his people, that was something he could never do. The religious situation had reached an impasse.

Nevertheless, help from the West gradually began to arrive.[8] If it was not so much as Constantine had hoped for, every bit was welcome. Pope Nicholas, realizing the emperor's efforts on behalf of the union, sent a troop of about two hundred mercenaries under command of Cardinal Isidore, a Byzantine who had returned to Italy not long after the Council of Florence and had risen to great prominence in the Catholic Church. Many of the inhabitants of Constantinople looked upon the cardinal as a renegade of the worst sort and considered him worse than no help at all. More enthusiasm greeted the dynamic soldier of fortune, Giovanni Giustiniani, who came from Genoa with a band of about five hundred crossbowmen. Venice, too, sent volunteers, and the presence on the same side of Venetians and Genoese, perennial enemies of each other, would mean a further problem for the emperor. So bitter was the hatred between these two Italian states, that even after the Turkish siege of the city began, their men sometimes forgot they were fighting in a common cause and fell to squabbling among themselves.

It was early in April 1453 that the Sultan Mehmet's forces began the formal siege of the city. The defenders soon discovered that the sultan possessed more sophisticated weaponry than any would-be conqueror before him. His particular pride was his bronze cannons, including one gigantic monster with a barrel over twenty-six feet long. This formidable weapon, and many smaller pieces, were the productions of a Christian artillery expert, Urban the Hungarian. Urban had earlier offered his services to the Emperor Constantine, but when the Byzantine sovereign was unable to pay the wages he demanded, the Hungarian departed for the employ of the Turks.[9]

Most of the sultan's forces were concentrated along the four-mile stretch of the great land walls. Day after day, Turkish artillerymen bombarded sections of the outer wall from across the foss. Mehmet's smaller cannons were proving more effective than the twenty-six-foot piece, which was so unwieldy it could be fired only seven times a day. While these operations went on, other Turks were engaged in an effort to fill up portions of the foss, so the cannons might be brought within closer range. For the Byzantine defenders, the principal activity thus far consisted in constant repair of the outer wall. Each night found hundreds of unlikely volunteers pitching in to aid the regular forces: monks, women, even young children. At last, after so many months of bickering, the sense of a common cause was beginning to be felt among at least some of the people of the city. Almost every morning, the emperor toured the walls, spoke encouragingly to the defenders, mediated squabbles between Greeks and Latins, Venetians and Genoese. Constantine was an optimistic man, and though he realized fully the gravity of the situation, he was determined to keep alive the hope of his people. His presence was felt everywhere: strong, calm, and unafraid.

On April 18, 1453, the Turks tried their first large-scale assault on the outer wall, charging over a section of the filled-in foss and throwing their siege ladders against the city's fortifications. After several hours of hard fighting, the Christians repelled the enemy. The Turks withdrew to their own lines, leaving about two hundred dead behind them, while the defenders of Constantinople reported that not even one of their own men had been killed.[10]

Two days later, another event occurred which caused the hopes of the besieged city to rise even higher. Three Genoese ships, full of munitions and foodstuffs sent by Pope Nicholas, approached the city together with an imperial transport ship that Constantine had sent out months earlier on the quest for Western aid. As the four vessels approached the Golden Horn, they were set upon by the Turkish fleet and for several hours a fierce battle raged. At length, the superior seamanship of the Christians combined with a fortunate gust of wind to produce a devastating setback for the Turks. While excited, ecstatically happy Byzantines watched from the sea-wall above the harbor, the four ships eluded their attackers, the boom was lifted and the vessels entered safe waters.[11]

The Sultan Mehmet reacted to the episode with characteristic vigor. Not only did he relieve the Turkish admiral of his command, the sultan almost beat the unfortunate man to death with his own hands, before sending him into exile. Turning next to more positive matters, since his fleet was obviously unable to get past the boom, Mehmet was determined that an alternate plan for getting his ships into the Golden Horn must be carried out. The proposal, which he had had under study for some time now, seemed incredible: he would have the ships dragged overland, behind Pera. Those who knew Mehmet knew better than to tell him it could not be done. The following day found the sultan's men building "wheeled cradles" to carry the Turkish fleet on its overland voyage.

On the morning of April 22, at the crack of dawn, the first of the Turkish vessels was eased upon its wheeled cradle and dragged ashore. Teams of oxen pulled the ships over the ground while hundreds of the sultan's men walked along the vessels to steady them over rough spots. For the Turks this almost miraculous journey of about seventy vessels across dry land called for joyous merrymaking. Musicians accompanying the procession provided stirring tunes on fife, trumpet, and drum, while Turkish banners flew defiantly in the breeze. Aboard each of the ships, the sailors waved their oars in the air. Sultan Mehmet was doing the impossible; and cold and cruel though he was, his men idolized him.

By noon, the first of the Turkish ships slipped into the waters of the Golden Horn. Horrified Byzantines watched from the sea-wall, where only two days earlier they had witnessed the unexpected triumph of the four Christian vessels. With the sultan's fleet in the Golden Horn, the defenders would have to spread their already thin ranks to protect the wall on this side of the city.[12] Those who remembered their history could recall ominously that in 1204 the crusaders penetrated the city on the side by the Golden Horn.

Meanwhile, Constantine called for an emergency meeting with the Venetian mercenary captains to discuss the new crisis. A clever plan was formulated: under cover of night, two small Venetian boats would venture out and set fire to the Turkish ships in the harbor, while several larger Venetian ships were designated to go along for protection. It was an excellent plan and might well have succeeded, had word of it not reached the Genoese. Enraged that their rivals, the Venetians, were assigned a starring role in what promised to be a gallant enterprise, they demanded the right to participate and thereby share the glory.

The proposed attack was postponed for several nights to allow for Genoese participation. The delay, as it turned out, was fatal; there was a security leak. Probably a Genoese sailor who learned of the plan passed along the word to a fellow Genoese in Pera, who informed the sultan. When the Christian fire-ships sailed, the Turks, who were waiting for them, opened fire. Two Christian vessels were sunk; the others escaped with heavy damage, while the Turkish fleet remained virtually unharmed.[13]

It was a serious setback for the defenders of Constantinople. Moreover, the Venetians and the Genoese blamed each other for the failure of the mission, and it seemed that actual warfare might break out between the two groups of volunteers. Constantine assembled a gathering of officers from both Italian states and addressed them with a stirring plea for cooperation. The tone of the emperor's message, if not his exact words, is preserved: "I pray you, my brethren, be of one mind and work together. Is it not enough misery that we have to fight against such fearful odds outside the walls? . . . Let us not have any conflicts amongst ourselves within the walls!"[14]

Hope was fading in the city. Food supplies were running low, and even the emperor began to feel strongly the growing desolation that hung over his people. It was about this time that the sultan, apprised of the situation in the besieged city, sent a message to Constantine demanding unconditional surrender. Mehmet added that Constantine might retire unharmed and would be compensated with a fief elsewhere. As for the city, Mehmet promised vaguely to be "merciful," but to those who had already experienced the sultan's failure to keep his word, these promises seemed absolutely futile. Constantine's advisors were strongly determined to carry on the defense of the city. Many of them, however, felt that the emperor should attempt escape. Constantine rejected such suggestions vigorously. One chronicler who wrote some time after the siege has captured the emperor's spirit in the speech he attributes to him: "I thank all for the advice which you have given me. I know that my going out of the city might be of some benefit to me. . . . But it is impossible for me to go away! How could I leave. . . my people in such a plight? I pray you, my friends, in the future do not say anything else but 'Nay, sire, do not leave us!' Never, never will I leave you! I am resolved to die here with you!"

"And saying this," the chronicler continues, "the emperor turned his head aside, because his eyes filled with tears; and with him wept . . . all who were there!"[15]

The Byzantines had always been an emotional people who saw no reason why a man need be ashamed to weep in times of sorrow. Constantine Palaiologos was a strong man; no one who knew him and fought for him ever doubted his courage and manliness. Yet through the trying weeks when he watched his nation falling and the reality of the role in which history had cast him became increasingly clear, the emperor's eyes would often fill with unashamed tears. There was little to do now but wait and pray.

22

The Twenty-ninth of May

As the long weeks of the siege wore on, the emperor still refused to resign himself wholly to the idea that the city was doomed. In his daily tours of the walls, he would often speak of the idea that if God willed it, the city might yet be saved. Nor was such optimism completely groundless. There were encouraging rumors from time to time: Venice reportedly was sending additional aid (actually the Venetian Senate was "considering" it, nothing more). More substance attached to reports that Mehmet was growing discouraged. Although weeks of heavy bombardment had leveled portions of the outer wall, the Turks had failed to inflict really extensive damage on the inner fortifications. Moreover, there was a strong peace party among the sultan's advisors urging him to lift the siege.

The young sultan, reluctant to give up the great enterprise, decided on one more all-out attack on the city. Should it fail, the Turks would indeed withdraw; should it succeed, the Byzantine Empire would be no more. The first step was a concerted effort to cover over the as yet unfilled portions of the foss outside the walls, in order to launch attacks simultaneously along the entire length of the land wall. When this task was completed, Mehmet ordered that May 28 should be a day of rest.[1]

165

Inside Constantinople the defenders realized clearly what was happening. In the face of the crucial attack about to come, religious differences were—almost—forgotten. A procession was formed; the holiest icons were brought out from their shrines and carried around the city. Practically everyone who could be spared from the immediate defense of the walls joined the procession, along with the emperor and his officials. Then as it ended, Constantine addressed his people with a brief, impromptu speech. The Byzantines, he said, had always believed that a man must be ready to die for his faith, his country, his family, or his emperor. Now they must be prepared to die for all four causes, and as for himself, he was ready to die with his people and for the city he so deeply loved. Constantine added that if he had ever offended anyone among his listeners, he prayed they would forgive him. It was practically impossible to listen to the emperor's calm and heroic words and not be deeply moved. His audience, Greeks and Latins alike, responded with brave shouts that they were ready to give their lives for him.[2]

Later that evening, from all over the city vast crowds of people converged upon Hagia Sophia. There Orthodox and Catholic priests joined in a celebration of the sacred rites; for once the union was a reality, in this last Christian service ever celebrated in Hagia Sophia. The emperor was present and remained long in prayer, stretched out on the cold floor before the holy iconostasis.

Then, following the services at Hagia Sophia, Constantine returned briefly to Blachernai Palace to address the members of his household staff. We do not know what the night will bring forth, he told them. The emperor's voice was filled with emotion but it was clear that he was resolved to face whatever came with unshakable courage. It was nearly midnight when with Sphrantzes and a few more of his most trusted colleagues, he left the palace for a tour of the walls. At many points along the way, Constantine stopped to speak to the defenders, to let them know he was there and that when the time came he would be fighting at their side.

When he reached the Caligarian Gate at the northwest corner of the city, he dismounted and with Sphrantzes climbed up to the top of the watchtower that stood at this crucial post. Below them, in one direction lay the waters of the Golden Horn, in the other, the lines of Turkish besiegers. Ominous lights flickered in the enemy camp, and ominous sounds could be heard: the Turks dragging their heavy artillery across the filled-in foss. For what seemed hours, but in reality cannot have been nearly so long, Constantine and Sphrantzes waited and watched in silence; then the emperor bade his friend farewell and returned to his own post at the gate of St. Romanos.[3]

A little before two o'clock in the morning, the Turkish assault began.[4]

There followed in the next hours one of the great battles of history. Wave after wave of Turkish troops approached the walls with scaling ladders only to be repulsed by the shower of arrows, stones, and Greek fire hurled down by the city's defenders. But for every Turk who fell, it seemed there were a hundred more to replace him. Still it was several hours before the first Turks gained a foothold on the wall.

Meanwhile Mehmet's cannons had been pounding away at selected weak spots in the fortifications and now other forces of the sultan entered through the shattered outer walls near the gate of St. Romanos. As fighting grew more intense, Giustiniani, the heroic Genoese captain, was struck—probably in the hand—by an arrow. In intense pain, he asked leave of the emperor to go and have his wound attended. Reluctantly, Constantine gave him a key leading from the inner wall to the city, and the Genoese captain withdrew. His departure caused widespread consternation among his men; seeing him depart and not knowing the cause, they ran after him. Panic spread among the defenders: the city is lost. . . . Before Giustiniani could have the gate closed, many had followed him inside Constantinople.[5]

But despite the flight of Giustiniani and many of the Genoese, on the walls most of Constantinople's defenders fought courageously on. In these last desperate hours, a sudden strange foreboding seized the emperor: he was not afraid to die, but he did not want the enemy to find and desecrate his body. Impulsively he tore off his imperial ornaments. Let there be nothing to distinguish the body of Constantine Palaiologos from that of any other soldier. . . . Still there were his red boots, those red shoes that only the basileus might wear, with the Palaiologos eagles tooled into the leather. Those he could not dispose of. It was as if fate had decreed that some mark of his emperorship must remain on him to the last.

There are many stories told of the emperor's courage in his final hours. When his horse was slain under him, he fought on on foot, wounded yet heedless of pain, heedless of anything but the grim reality that here in the grey predawn of this May morning, his beloved nation was falling and that he must die with it. We do not know precisely how he was slain, yet we can be sure that he died as bravely as he had lived.[6]

By afternoon of the same day, May 29, 1453, the Sultan Mehmet the Conqueror entered Constantinople in triumph. As his troops indulged in the three days of unrestrained looting he had promised them, Mehmet concerned himself with seeking positive assurance that Constantine was dead and ordered a search for the body of the fallen emperor among the heaps of the slain. According to several sources, it was as Constantine had feared: in vain had he cast off the other insignia of his office, for by his red boots, they identified him. The body was beheaded and many Byzantines who witnessed their fallen sovereign's head on public display affirmed that this was indeed Constantine, and wept openly at the sight.[7] Those who remained alive, who had somehow survived the fall of the empire and who would have to keep on living—perhaps as slaves of Turkish masters—could look back on their emperor in a different light now. Forgotten were the troubles over the union of the churches; forgotten the lack of cooperation with which many had greeted his efforts. To be remembered only was the fact that a good and courageous man had given his life for his people. Legends flowered among the latter-day Greeks. He was not dead, they said; an angel had whisked him away and hidden him in an underground cavern where he lay sleeping until the day when he would rise again to free his people from the oppressor.

And still, the city he loved and for which he died lived on—the same, yet profoundly, unalterably changed. In time even the name "Constantinople," as much a memorial to him as to the first Constantine, would give place to "Istanbul." The Byzantine Empire, the land of the Palaiologoi, is a vanished world, receding with the passing of centuries ever farther into the dim reaches of the historical past. Still the memory of Constantine Dragases Palaiologos endures, a symbol of all that was best and finest in the Byzantine spirit. Could any nation wish a finer memorial than this?

Notes

Chapter 2

1. Demetrios I. Polemis, *The Doukai* (London, 1968), pp. 106–108.

2. George Pachymeres, *De Michaele et Andronico Palaeologo,* ed. I. Bekker, 2 vols. (Bonn, 1835), I, 127.

3. Deno John Geanakoplos, *Emperor Michael Palaeologus and the West: 1258–1282* (Cambridge, Mass., 1959), p. 19.

4. Michael VIII, *Imperatoris Michaelis Palaeologi de vita sua opusculum necnon regulae quam ipse monasterio S. Demetrii praescripsit fragmentum,* ed. J. Troitsky (St. Petersburg, 1885), p. 3. Also to be found more accessibly in Henri Grégoire, ed. and trans., "Imperatoris Michaelis Palaeologi De Vita Sua," *Byzantion,* 29–30 (1959-60), 452. See also, Geanakoplos, *Michael,* p. 19, n.13.

5. George Akropolites, *Opera,* ed. A. Heisenberg, 2 vols. (Leipzig, 1903), I, 95–96. For Michael's ordeal see also, Nikephoros Gregoras, *Bizantina historia,* ed. L. Schopen and I. Bekker, 3 vols. (Bonn, 1829-1845), I, 49; Geanakoplos, *Michael,* pp. 22–25; Alice Gardner, *The Lascarids of Nicaea* (London, 1912; reprint Chicago, 1967), pp. 189–191.

6. Polemis, *The Doukai,* p. 3.

7. Akropolites, I, 134.

8. Geanakoplos, *Michael,* p. 31, n. 61, quoting a letter of Theodore Laskaris to Nikephoros Vlemmydes.

9. For details see Pachymeres, I, 33–35.

10. For details see Donald M. Nicol, "The Fourth Crusade and the Greek and Latin Empires," *The Cambridge Medieval History,* vol. IV, pt. 1, ed. Joan M. Hussey (Cambridge, England, 1966), pp. 322–324; George Ostrogorsky, *History of the Byzantine State,* second English ed., trans. Joan M. Hussey (Oxford, 1968), pp. 445–446. The long and complicated history of the independent Epirote state is studied in depth in D. M. Nicol, *The Despotate of Epiros* (Oxford, 1957).

11. Pachymeres, I, 31–35.

12. Ibid., pp. 55–62.

13. Ibid., p. 62.

Chapter 3

1. Pachymeres, I, 101–104.

2. For details on the Treaty of Nymphaion, see Geanakoplos, *Michael,* pp. 84–89.

3. Geanakoplos, *Michael,* pp. 119–120.

4. Gregoras, I, 88.

5. Pachymeres, I, 162.

6. Ibid., p. 188. See also, Geanakoplos, *Michael,* pp. 124–125.

7. Pachymeres, I, 191–192; Gregoras, I, 93.

8. Geanakoplos, *Michael,* pp. 217–218. Geanakoplos, however, expresses doubt that John escaped, since the Greek historians Pachymeres and Gregoras both report that he was still a prisoner years later when he was visited by Michael's son, Andronikos II.

9. Polemis, *The Doukai,* p. 111.

10. A detailed and interesting study of the international schemes of Charles of Anjou with due attention to Michael's role in his eventual defeat is Steven

Runciman, *The Sicilian Vespers* (Cambridge, England, 1958).

11. Pachymeres, I, 379.

12. Geanakoplos, *Michael,* p. 342.

13. *Imperatoris Michaelis . . . opusculum,* p. 9; (Grégoire, "De Vita Sua," p. 462). See also Geanakoplos, *Michael,* p. 367.

14. Pachymeres, I, 524–528.

15. For details see D. M. Nicol, "The Byzantine Reaction to the Second Council of Lyons, 1274," in *Byzantium: Its Ecclesiastical History and Relations with the Western World* (London, 1972), pp. 137–138.

16. Apostolos E. Vacalopoulos, *Origins of the Greek Nation,* trans. Ian Moles (New Brunswick, N. J., 1970), p. 40.

Chapter 4

1. The best portrait of Andronikos II is that found in Codex Monacensis Ms. Gr. 442, now in the Staatsbibliothek in Munich. The well-known series of imperial portraits in Codex α. S. 5. 5 in the Biblioteca Estense, Modena, Italy, also contains a portrait of Andronikos II featuring—almost caricaturing—his unusual beard.

2. Pachymeres, I, 468. See also, Angeliki E. Laiou, *Constantinople and the Latins: The Foreign Policy of Andronicus II: 1282-1328* (Cambridge, Mass., 1972), p. 24.

3. Gregoras, I, 174; Pachymeres, II, 69–71.

4. Gregoras, I, 317.

5. On the size of the company, which varies widely in the sources, see Laiou, *Constantinople,* p. 134; Kenneth M. Setton, *Catalan Domination of Athens* (Cambridge, Mass., 1948), p. 3.

6. For details see Alfonso Lowe, *The Catalan Vengeance* (London, 1972), pp. 22–23.

7. Lowe, *Catalan Vengeance,* pp. 56–57.

8. Ibid., pp. 62–63, examines conflicting data on Roger's death in the various sources.

9. For the subsequent history of the Catalans, see the concluding chapters of Lowe, Catalan Vengeance, and more particularly the important and detailed monograph of Setton, Catalan Domination of Athens.

Chapter 5

1. On Yolande of Montferrat see the biographical sketch in Charles Diehl, Byzantine Empresses, trans. Harold Bell and Theresa de Kerpely (New York, 1963), pp. 276–286.

2. Pachymeres, II, 276–277.

3. For details see William Miller, "The Medieval Serbian Empire" in Essays on the Latin Orient (Amsterdam, 1964), p. 448.

4. Gregoras, I, 243.

5. Ibid., pp. 273–275; 293.

6. Ibid., p. 235. See also John W. Barker, "The Problem of Appanages in Byzantium during the Palaiologan Period," Byzantina, 3 (1971), 105–108.

7. On the date, see Laiou, Constantinople, p. 230, n. 123.

8. For more details on the Marquis Teodoro, see Angeliki E. Laiou, "A Byzantine Prince Latinized," Byzantion, 38 (1968), 386–410.

9. Diehl, Byzantine Empresses, p. 286.

Chapter 6

1. Or perhaps 1296. See Ursula V. Bosch, Kaiser Andronikos III Palaiologos: Versuch einer Darstellung der byzantinischen Geschichte in den Jahren 1321-1341 (Amsterdam, 1965), p. 7; Averikos Th. Papadopulos, Versuch einer Genealogie der Palaiologen: 1259-1453 (Munich, 1938, reprint Amsterdam, 1962), p. 43.

2. For the evidence that John Kantakouzenos was a posthumous child, see Donald M. Nicol, The Byzantine

Family of Kantakouzenos (Washington, 1968, pp. 27–30; 35–36.

    3.   Diehl, *Byzantine Empresses*, p. 292.

    4.   Gregoras, I, 320–321.

    5.   For details, see Gregoras, I, 284–286. Kantakouzenos in his history (I, 13–14) hurries over this incident since it was so much to the discredit of his friend Andronikos. See also, Bosch, *Andronikos III*, p. 14.

    6.   Gregoras, I, 284–286; John Kantakouzenos, *Historiarum libri IV*, 3 vols., ed. L. Schopen and B. G. Niebuhr (Bonn, 1828–1832), I, 13–14.

Chapter 7

    1.   Kantakouzenos, I, 138.

    2.   Gregoras, I, 293–295; Kantakouzenos, I, 14–16.

    3.   Gregoras, I, 295–296; Kantakouzenos, I, 16–23.

    4.   For details, see Laiou, *Constantinople*, p. 284.

    5.   Kantakouzenos, I, 56–92; Gregoras, I, 312–316. See also, Edwin Pears, *The Destruction of the Greek Empire and the Story of the Capture of Constantinople by the Turks* (1903, reprint New York, 1968), pp. 67–68; Valentin Parisot, *Cantacuzène, homme d' état et historien* (Paris, 1845), pp. 42–47.

    6.   Kantakouzenos, I, 84–89.

    7.   Gregoras, I, 319.

    8.   Kantakouzenos, I, 196–204.

    9.   Gregoras, I, 373.

Chapter 8

    1.   On Anne of Savoy, see Diehl's essay in his *Byzantine Empresses*, pp. 287–308.

    2.   As Laiou points out, *Constantinople*, p. 302, there were family ties between Savoy and Montferrat and it was probably Andronikos II's Italianized son, the Marquis Teodoro, who recommended the match.

    3.   Kantakouzenos, I, 205.

4. To have appeared before the emperor bareheaded would have been considered unspeakably rude by the Byzantines of the late empire.

5. Gregoras, I, 566-567. For more detail see also, Ihor Ševčenko, "The Decline of Byzantium Seen Through the Eyes of Its Intellectuals," *Dumbarton Oaks Papers,* 15 (1961), 182.

6. Gregoras, I, 383–384; Kantakouzenos, I, 193–208.

7. Gregoras, I, 415–428.

8. Ibid, pp. 423–424; the translation is that of Laiou, *Constantinople,* pp. 297–298.

Chapter 9

1. Kantakouzenos, I, 335–337.

2. For details see Nicol, *Kantakouzenos,* p. 41; Bosch, *Andronikos III,* pp. 152–158.

3. Kantakouzenos, I, 363–370.

4. Ibid., p. 393.

5. On the birthdate of the future John V, see John W. Barker, *Manuel II Palaeologus, 1391–1425: A Study in Late Byzantine Statesmanship* (New Brunswick, N. J., 1969), p. 81, n. 214. Other authorities place his birth in November, 1331. Cf. *Cambridge Medieval History,* IV, i, 356, n. 2.

6. Kantakouzenos, I, 504.

7. Papadopulos, *Versuch einer Genealogie der Palaiologen,* p. 43.

8. Diehl, *Byzantine Empresses,* p. 294.

9. Kantakouzenos, I, 557–560.

Chapter 10

1. For details, see Nicol, *Kantakouzenos,* p. 44.

2. Peter Charanis' important article, "Internal Strife in Byzantium during the Fourteenth Century," *Byzantion,* 15 (1940–41), 208–230, emphasizes the element of class struggle in the conflict between Anne and Kantakouzenos.

3. Diehl, *Byzantine Empresses,* p. 296.

4. Kantakouzenos, II, 166–167; Gregoras, II, 599–605.

5. Kantakouzenos, II, 582; Gregoras, II, 762–765.
6. Kantakouzenos, II, 564–568; Gregoras, II, 762.
7. Nicol, *Kantakouzenos*, p. 62.
8. Kantakouzenos, II, 602–615.
9. Gregoras, III, 199.
10. Gregoras, II, 788.

Chapter 11

1. Gregoras, II, 790.
2. Kantakouzenos, III, 80.
3. For more detail see Donald M. Nicol, *The Last Centuries of Byzantium* (New York, 1972), pp. 227–232.
4. Kantakouzenos, III, 49–52.
5. Kantakouzenos, III, 162–165.
6. Ms. grec. 1242, f. 5v., Bibliothèque Nationale, Paris.
7. Kantakouzenos, III, 200–209.
8. Kantakouzenos, III, 250–254.
9. Kantakouzenos, III, 275–276.
10. Doukas, *Istoria Turco-bizantina,* ed. V. Grecu (Bucharest, 1958), pp. 67–71. English translation by Harry J. Magoulias, *Decline and Fall of Byzantium to the Ottoman Turks* (Detroit, 1975), pp. 77–79. Donald M. Nicol, "The Abdication of John Cantacuzene," *Byzantinische Forschungen,* 2 (Amsterdam, 1967), 274–279, casts some doubt on the particulars of Doukas' story.
11. Parisot, *Cantacuzène,* p. 298.
12. Kantakouzenos, III, 304–308.
13. Nicol, *Kantakouzenos*, p. 94.
14. Ibid., p. 107.
15. Philotheos quoted by J. Meyendorf, "Projets de Concile oecuménique en 1367: un dialogue inédit entre Jean Cantacuzène et le légat Paul," *Dumbarton Oaks Papers,* 14 (1960), 150.
16. Nicol, *Kantakouzenos*, p. 89.
17. Nicol, *Last Centuries,* p. 245.
18. In many older works it is stated erroneously that

Kantakouzenos retired to Mt. Athos. For details see Nicol, *Kantakouzenos*, pp. 92–94.

19. Gregoras, quoted in Diehl, *Byzantine Empresses*, p. 293.

Chapter 12

1. With the reign of the adult John V, Byzantine history enters a period in which contemporary historical literature is sadly deficient; there is nothing to compare with the earlier works of such writers as Akropolites, Pachymeres, and Gregoras. Short monastic chronicles and the works of the later historians Doukas and Chalkokondyles help somewhat to fill the gap, but these are frequently unreliable. Consequently, the monographic work of modern Byzantinists utilizing obscure documentary material, letters, and so on is of particular importance here.

2. On Andronikos' birthdate, April 11, 1348, see Barker, *Manuel II*, p. 5, n. 8.

3. Letter of Manuel Palaiologos to Alexios Iagoup, quoted by George T. Dennis, *The Reign of Manuel II Palaeologus in Thessalonica* (Rome, 1960), p. 14. See also Barker, *Manuel*, pp. 410–413.

4. The basic monograph on John's dealings with the West and his conversion is Oscar Halecki, *Un Empereur de Byzance à Rome: Vingt ans de travail pour l'union des églises et pour la défense de l'empire d'orient, 1355-1373* (Warsaw, 1930). See also Louis Bréhier, *Le Monde byzantin*, I (Paris, 1947), 454–456.

5. For details see Halecki, *Un Empereur*, pp. 24–31; Barker, *Manuel*, pp. 4–5.

6. Among the important monographs dealing with John's Venetian visit are: Oscar Halecki, "Two Palaeologi in Venice, 1370–1371," *Byzantion*, 17 (1944–45), 331–335; Raymond-J. Loenertz, O. P., "Jean V Paléologue à Venise (1370–1371)," *Revue des études byzantines*, 16 (1958), 217–232; J. Chrysostomides, "John V Palaeologus in Venice (1370–1371) and the Chronicle of Caroldo: a Rein-

terpretation," *Orientalia Christiana Periodica*, 31 (1965), 76–84.

7. Tenedos, however, was not actually turned over to Venice until 1373. See Chrysostomides, "John V in Venice," *O. C. P.*, 31 (1965), 79.

Chapter 13

1. For a detailed analysis of the sources see Raymond-J. Loenertz, "La première insurrection d'Andronic Paléologue (1373)," *Échos d' orient*, 38 (1939), 334–345.

2. Loenertz, "La première insurrection," *Échos d' orient*, 38 (1939), 335–336.

3. For details in addition to Loenertz, see Barker, *Manuel*, pp. 21–22.

4. Ruy González de Clavijo, *Embassy to Tamerlane: 1403–1406*, trans. Guy Le Strange (London, 1928), p. 86.

5. Clavijo, *Embassy*, p. 86.

6. Barker, *Manuel*, pp. 28–29.

7. Dennis, *Manuel*, p. 15, n. 45.

8. From a letter of Manuel to Alexios Iagoup quoted by Barker, *Manuel*, p. 412.

9. Jacopo Zeno, *La Vita di Carlo Zeno, Gran Capitano de' Viniziani* (Venice, 1858), pp. 37–40. See also Barker, *Manuel*, pp. 458–460.

10. For details see Nicol, *Kantakouzenos*, p. 137.

11. Barker, *Manuel*, p. 39.

Chapter 14

1. Quoted by Dennis, *Manuel*, p. 109.

2. Demetrios Kydones, Letter 342, quoted by Dennis, *Manuel*, p. 113

3. Manuel's "Funeral Oration for His Brother Theodore," quoted by Barker, *Manuel*, p. 402.

4. On this matter see John W. Barker, "John VII in Genoa: A Problem in Late Byzantine Source Confusion," *Orientalia Christiana Periodica*, 28 (1962), 213–238.

5. The basic monograph on the career of John VII is

Franz Dölger, "Johannes VII, Kaiser der Rhomäer, 1390–1408," *Byzantinische Zeitschrift*, 31 (1931), 21–36.

6.   The emperor's intention to change his name seems clear from the fact that he was officially hailed as "Andronikos." For details, see Barker, *Manuel*, pp. 73–74, n. 106.

7.   Quoted by A. A. Vasiliev, *History of the Byzantine Empire* (Madison, Wisc., 1958), pp. 587–588.

8.   Doukas (trans. Magoulias), p. 82.

9.   This story apparently originated with Laonikos Chalkokandyles, *Historiarum demonstrationes*, ed. E. Darko, 2 vols. (Budapest, 1922–27), I, 74–76. Chalkokandyles, who wrote in the late fifteenth century (after the fall of Constantinople) must be used with extreme caution for earlier events.

10.   As proved by Raymond-J. Loenertz, "Une erreur singulière de Laonic Chalcocandyle: Le prétendu second marriage de Jean V Paléologue," *Revue des Études Byzantines*, 15 (1957), 176–181. Even the usually reliable Papadopulos, *Versuch*, p. 46, errs on the matter of Eudokia.

Chapter 15

1.   George Sphrantzes, *Chronicon Minus*, ed. J.-P. Migne, *Patrologia Graeca*, vol. 156, col. 1030, A-B.

2.   Barker, *Manuel*, p. 402.

3.   P. Schreiner, ed., "Hochzeit und Krönung Kaiser Manuels II. im Jahre 1392," *Byzantinische Zeitschrift*, 60 (1967), 76–79. Translation by Charles M. Brand, *Icon and Minaret* (Englewood Cliffs, N. J., 1969), pp. 10–13. See also, F. E. Brightman, "Byzantine Imperial Coronations," *Journal of Theological Studies*, 2 (1901), 387–392.

4.   Now located in the Louvre, Paris (Ivoires, A 53, f. 1).

5.   Barker, *Manuel*, p. 402.

6.   For more detail on the Serres conference, see Barker, *Manuel*, pp. 114–121.

7.   For more detail, see Barker, *Manuel*, pp. 490–493.

Chapter 16

1. Quoted by Barker, *Manuel*, p. 494.
2. There are several monographs relating the story of Manuel's journey to the West with varying degrees of detail. E.g., M. Jugie, "Le voyage de l'empereur Manuel Paléologue en occident (1399–1403)," *Échos d'orient*, 15 (1912), 322–332; Gustave Schlumberger, "Un Empereur de Byzance à Paris et à Londres," *Byzance et Croisades* (Paris, 1927), pp. 87–147; H. C. Luke, "Visitors from the East to the Plantagenet and Lancastrian Kings," *Nineteenth Century*, 108 (1930), 767–769; and D. M. Nicol, "A Byzantine Emperor in England: Manuel II's Visit to London in 1400–1401," in *Byzantium: Its Ecclesiastical History and Relations with the Western World*, pp. 204–225.
3. Manuel's "Letter λζ´" to Manuel Chrysolaras, quoted in Barker, *Manuel*, p. 174.
4. Barker, *Manuel*, p. 397.
5. Adam of Usk, *Chronicle*, ed. E. M. Thompson (London, 1904), pp. 219–220.

Chapter 17

1. It is likely that John VII and his wife Evgenia Gattilusi had a son who had died in early childhood. For details see George T. Dennis, S. J., "An Unknown Byzantine Emperor, Andronikos V Palaeologus (1400–1407?)," *Jahrbuch der Österreichischen Byzantinischen Gessel-schaft*, 16 (1967), 175–187.
2. Manuel's "Letter ια´," quoted in Barker, *Manuel*, p. 415.
3. Manuel's "Letter μδ´," quoted in Barker, *Manuel*, p. 404.
4. Ibid.
5. Clavijo, *Embassy*, pp. 61–89.
6. Ibid., p. 61.
7. Ibid., pp. 62–80.

8. Ibid., pp. 87–88.

9. On this subject, see Barker, *Manuel,* pp. 298–319; the same author's article, "On the Chronology of the Activities of Manuel II Palaeologus in the Peloponnesus in 1415," *Byzantinische Zeitschrift,* 55 (1962), 39–55; and William Miller, *The Latins in the Levant* (London, 1908, reprint Cambridge, 1964), pp. 377–384.

10. Manuel's letter to the monks David and Damianos of Thessaloniki, quoted by Barker, *Manuel,* pp. 302–303.

11. Ibid., p. 303.

12. Sphrantzes, *Chronicon Minus,* col. 1047 A-B.

13. Ibid., col. 1029 A-B.

Chapter 18

1. Pero Tafur, *Travels and Adventures,* ed. and trans. Malcolm Lewis (London, 1926), p. 145.

2. Tafur, *Travels,* p. 117.

3. On Sophia see Charles Diehl, *Figures byzantines,* II ser. (Paris, 1908), 273–275.

4. For details see Doukas (trans. Magoulias), p. 113.

5. "The Travels of Bertrandon de La Brocquière," in *Early Travels in Palestine,* ed. and trans. Thomas Wright (London, 1848), pp. 338–339. See also Chedomil Mijatovich, *Constantine Palaeologus, The Last Emperor of the Greeks* (1892; reprint Chicago, 1968), p. 53.

6. La Brocquière in *Early Travels,* p. 341. See also Alexander A. Vasiliev, "La Guerre de cent ans et Jeanne d'Arc dans la tradition byzantine," *Byzantion,* 3 (1926), 241–250.

7. La Brocquière in *Early Travels,* p. 339.

8. Tafur, *Travels,* pp. 117–123. On Tafur see also the lengthy article of Alexander A. Vasiliev, "Pero Tafur, A Spanish Traveler of the Fifteenth Century and his Visit to Constantinople, Trebizond, and Italy," *Byzantion,* 7 (1932), 75–112.

9. Tafur, *Travels,* p. 145.

10. Ibid., p. 139.

Chapter 19

1. For details see Barker, *Manuel*, pp. 347–379.
2. Joseph Gill, S.J., *The Council of Florence* (Cambridge, England, 1959), p. 90. (Hereinafter cited as *Council*).
3. Gill, *Council*, pp. 89–91.
4. For details on John in Venice see Gill, *Council*, pp. 98–101; Diehl, *Figures byzantines*, II, 279–281.
5. Silvester Syropoulos, *Vera historia unionis non verae*, ed. R. Creyghton (Hagae-Comitis, 1660), p. 83.
6. Gill, *Council*, pp. 104–105.
7. Ibid., p. 127.
8. Letter of Nicholas Notaras quoted in Joseph Gill, S. J., *Personalities of the Council of Florence* (New York, 1964), p. 113. (Hereinafter cited as *Personalities*).
9. Tafur, *Travels*, pp. 174–176.
10. Syropoulos, *Vera historia*, pp. 167–168; see also Gill, *Council*, pp. 142–146.
11. For more details see Constantin Marinesco, "Deux empereurs byzantins: Manuel II et Jean VIII Paléologue vus par des artistes occidentaux," *Le Flambeau*, 40 (1957), 759–762.
12. Syropoulos, *Vera historia*, p. 235.
13. Steven Runciman, *The Fall of Constantinople* (Cambridge, England, 1969), p. 18.
14. Syropoulos, *Vera historia*, p. 329.
15. Ibid., p. 338.
16. Gill, *Personalities*, p. 124.

Chapter 20

1. The last Constantine is usually counted as number XI, though in some older works he is numbered XII, through mistaken enumeration of a nonexistent emperor, Constantine Laskaris, as Constantine XI.
2. Mijatovich, *Constantine*, p. 231.
3. Modern scholarship has shown conclusively that Sphrantzes was not the author of the often quoted *Chronicon*

Majus, but that it is in its present form the work of a sixteenth-century compiler, Makarios Melisennos. The *Chronicon Minus,* however, upon which portions of the *Majus* are based, is an authentic work of Sphrantzes. For details, see especially Raymond-J. Loenertz, "Autour de *Chronicon Maius* attribué à Georges Phrantzes," *Miscellanea* G. Mercati, III: *Letteratura e storia bizantina* (Studi e Testi, 123; Rome, 1946), 273–311. Unfortunately Sir Steven Runciman's *The Fall of Constantinople* fails to take sufficient account of this problem and thus must be used with caution in sections citing Sphrantzes. Nevertheless, as Margaret Carroll demonstrates in her important article, "Notes on the Authorship of the 'Siege Section' of the *Chronicon Maius* of Pseudo-Phrantzes, Book III, " *Byzantion,* 41 (1971), 28–44, there is considerable evidence that Melisennos used an expanded text of Sphrantzes (now lost), and that the siege material in the so-called "Pseudo-Phrantzes" is largely authentic.

4. Sphrantzes, *Chronicon Minus,* col. 1030 C.

5. For more detail see Miller, *The Latins in the Levant,* p. 388.

6. Codex α . S. 5. 5 (= Gr. 122), f. 294ˇ in the Biblioteca Estense, Modena, Italy.

7. For details see G. Kolias, "Constantin Paléologue, Le dernier défenseur de Constantinople," *L'Hellénisme contemporain,* special issue (Athens, 1953), pp. 42–43.

8. For details see Miller, *Essays on the Latin Orient,* p. 329.

9. Runciman, *Fall of Constantinople,* pp. 49–50; Nicol, *Last Centuries,* p. 368; Miller, *Latins in the Levant,* pp. 407–409.

10. Sphrantzes, *Chronicon Minus,* col. 1052 B. See also Nicol, *Last Centuries,* pp. 390-391.

11. Nicolò Barbaro, *Diary of the Siege of Constantinople,* trans. J. R. Jones (New York, 1969), p. 61.

12. Sphrantzes, *Chronicon Minus,* col. 1052 C.

13. Mijatovich, *Constantine*, pp. 125–126, quoting Pseudo-Phrantzes, *Chronicon Majus*.

14. Sphrantzes, *Chronicon Minus*, col. 1052 C-D.

15. For details see Ioannis A. Papadrianos, "The Marriage Arrangement between Constantine XI Palaeologus and the Serbian Mara," *Balkan Studies*, 6 (1965), 131–138.

16. Sphrantzes, *Chronicon Minus*, col. 1054 D–1055 A.

Chapter 21

1. For an excellent diagram of the city's fortifications see Philip Sherrard, *Byzantium* ("Great Ages of Man: Time-Life Books"; New York, 1966), pp. 90–91. See also, Runciman, *Fall*, pp. 89–91.

2. Doukas (trans. Magoulias), pp. 191–193; Runciman, *Fall*, p. 65.

3. Kritovoulos of Imbros. *History of Mehmed the Conqueror*, trans. Charles T. Riggs (Princeton, 1954; reprint Westport, Conn., 1969), pp. 16–18; Barbaro, *Diary*, pp. 9–10.

4. Sphrantzes, *Chronicon Minus*, col. 1061 A, actually states that there were only 200 foreigners but this is almost certainly an error for 2000. See also, Runciman, *Fall*, p. 85; Mijatovich, *Constantine*, pp. 141–142; Nicol, *Last Centuries*, p. 416, n. 17.

5. Kritovoulos, p. 36.

6. Quoted in Gill, *Personalities*, p. 123.

7. Doukas (trans. Magoulias), p. 210.

8. For details see Kritovoulos, pp. 39–40; Barbaro, p. 22.

9. Doukas (trans. Magoulias), p. 200; Kritovoulos, pp. 43–46; Runciman, *Fall*, pp. 77–78.

10. Kritovoulos, pp. 49–50; Barbaro, pp. 32–33; Runciman, *Fall*, p. 99.

11. Kritovoulos, pp. 53–55; Doukas (trans. Mag-

oulias), pp. 213–214; Barbaro, pp. 33–35; Runciman, *Fall,* pp. 100–103.

12. Kritovoulos, pp. 56–57; Barbaro, pp. 37–38.

13. Barbaro, pp. 38–42; Runciman, *Fall,* pp. 107–108.

14. Quoted in Mijatovich, *Constantine,* pp. 168–169, from the *Chronicon Majus* of Pseudo-Phrantzes, p. 258.

15. *The Slavonic Chronicle,* quoted in Mijatovich, *Constantine,* pp. 173–174.

Chapter 22

1. Kritovoulos, p. 66.

2. Runciman, *Fall,* pp. 130–131, paraphrasing an account by the Archbishop Leonard of Chios, an eyewitness.

3. Runciman, *Fall,* p. 132.

4. Barbaro, p. 62.

5. Kritovoulos, p. 70; Barbaro, p. 65.

6. For an interesting presentation of later Greek folklore and legend on Constantine's death and the fall of the city, see G. Megas, "La Prise de Constantinople dans la poésie et la tradition populaires grecques," *L'Hellénisme contemporain,* special issue (Athens, 1953). See also Kritovoulos, p. 82; Barbaro, p. 68; and Speros Vryonis, *The Decline of Medieval Hellenism in Asia Minor* (Berkeley, 1971), pp. 437–438.

7. Runciman, *Fall,* pp. 143–144, examines various accounts of the fate of Constantine's body, apparently with some doubt that the corpse identified as the emperor's was really his.

Selected
Bibliography

I.   MAJOR EARLY SOURCES (in approximate chronological order)

Very few of the primary sources for the Palaiologan period are available in English translation. The following bibliography indicates English editions where these exist as well as the texts in their original languages.

Akropolites, George. *Opera.* Edited by A. Heisenberg. 2 vols. Leipzig, 1903. Vol. 1. Akropolites (1217–1282) was a contemporary and close acquaintance of Theodore Laskaris II and Michael VIII. The best source for most of the Nicaean period and the early years of the restored empire in Constantinople.
Palaiologos, Michael VIII. *Imperatoris Michaelis Palaeologi de vita sua opusculum necnon regulae quam ipse monasterio S. Demetrii praescripsit fragmentum.* Edited by J. Troitskii. St. Petersburg, 1885. Greek text with French translation also appears in Henri Grégoire, ed., "Imperatoris Michaelis Palaeologi: De Vita Sua," *Byzantion* 29–30 (1959–60), 447–475.
Pachymeres, George. *De Michaele et Andronico Palaeologis.* Edited by I. Bekker. 2 vols. Bonn, 1835.

Pachymeres (1242–1307?) is the continuator of the *History* of Akropolites, and is an important source both for the reign of Michael VIII (whom he disliked) and the first half of the reign of Andronikos II.

Gregoras, Nikephoros. *Bizantina historia.* Edited by L. Schopen and I. Bekker. 3 vols. Bonn, 1829–1855. Gregoras (c. 1295–1360) was a close friend of Andronikos II and is one of the most important sources for the civil wars of the Andronikoi and the later struggles of Kantakouzenos and Anne of Savoy.

Kantakouzenos, John Joasaph. *Historiarum libri IV.* Edited by L. Schopen and B. G. Niebuhr. 3 vols. Bonn, 1828–1832. Kantakouzenos wrote this lengthy history of his life and reign after his abdication. Although he is unquestionably biased in his own favor, modern Byzantinists tend to regard his work as generally reliable.

Palaiologos, Manuel II. *Correspondence: Lettres de l'empereur Manuel Paléologue.* Edited by E. Legrand. Paris, 1893, reprint 1962. Greek text of most of the Emperor Manuel's letters. English translations of a number of these, in whole or part, are to be found in the monographs of Barker and Dennis cited below.

Clavijo, Ruy González de. *Embassy to Tamerlane: 1403–1406.* Translated by Guy Le Strange. London, 1928. Spanish text: *Embajada a Tamorlan.* Edited by F. López Estrada. Madrid, 1943. Contains an interesting description of Constantinople at the time of Clavijo's visit in the early fifteenth century.

Zeno, Jacopo. *La Vita di Carlo Zeno, Gran Capitano de' Viniziani.* Venice, 1858. Italian bishop Zeno's story of the adventures of his kinsman Carlo, includes an account of Carlo's attempt to rescue John V.

La Brocquière, Bertrandon de. "The Travels of Bertrandon de La Brocquière," *Early Travels in Palestine.* Edited and translated by Thomas Wright. French text: *Le Voyage d'Outremer.* Edited by C. H. A. Schefer. Paris, 1892. Has

a few interesting pages on the Burgundian La Brocquière's visit to Constantinople in the reign of John VIII.
Tafur, Pero. *Travels and Adventures: 1435–1439.* Edited and
translated by Malcolm Letts. London, 1926. Spanish
text: *Andanças é Viajes de Pero Tafur por diversas
partes del mundo avidos.* Edited by D. Marcos Jiménez
de la Espada. Madrid, 1874. Contains lively recollections of Pero's visits to his "cousin" John VIII in
Constantinople and Italy.
Syropoulos, Silvester. *Vera Historia unionis non verae.*
Edited by R. Creyghton. Hagae-Comitis, 1660. The most
detailed narrative of the Council of Florence by a Greek
delegate who strongly opposed the union of the
churches.
Barbaro, Nicolò. *Diary of the Siege of Constantinople.*
Translated by J. R. Jones. New York, 1969. Italian text:
Giornale dell' assedio di Constantinopli. Edited by E.
Cornet. Vienna, 1856. Barbaro, a Venetian surgeon, was
present during the siege of Constantinople in 1453. His
diary, reconstructed not long afterwards, is a generally
reliable account.
Sphrantzes, George. *Chronicon Minus.* Edited by J.-P.
Migne. *Patrologia Graeca,* vol. 156, coll. 1025–1080.
George Sphrantzes' authentic work, *Chronicon Minus,*
seems short and rather disappointing compared with
the more detailed *Chronicon Maius,* long ascribed to him
but now recognized as largely the work of a sixteenth-
century compiler. The *Minus* is important nonetheless
for Sphrantzes' first-hand acquaintance with Manuel II,
John VIII, and Constantine XI.
Kritovoulos of Imbros, Michael. *History of Mehmed the
Conqueror.* Translated by Charles T. Riggs. Princeton,
1954, reprint Westport, Conn., 1970. Greek text:
Historiai. Edited by V. Grecu. Bucharest, 1963. Kritovoulos' history of the siege of Constantinople and
subsequent victories of the Turks to 1467 was dedicated
to the sultan himself. While Kritovoulos was not

personally present during the siege in 1453 his account
is fair, unbiased, and based on generally reliable
research.

Chalkokondyles, Laonikos. *Historiarum demonstrationes*.
Edited by E. Darkó. 2 vols. Budapest, 1922–1927. The
work of the Athenian Chalkokondyles, written probably in the 1480's, must be used with extreme caution as it
contains numerous mistakes.

Doukas (Michael?). *Istoria turco-bizantina: 1341–1462*.
Edited by V. Grecu. Bucharest, 1958. English translation
by Harry J. Magoulias, *The Decline and Fall of
Byzantium to the Ottoman Turks*. Detroit, 1975. Like
Chalkokondyles, Doukas, who wrote in the late fifteenth century, is an important source, but is not
completely reliable.

II. USEFUL MODERN WORKS

No attempt is made here to catalogue the vast
monographic literature in many languages on the Palaiologan period. The following bibliography provides rather a
list of some of the principal books and monographs most
likely to be useful to the interested reader who wishes to
undertake further reading in the Palaiologan epoch. For
this reason, heaviest emphasis is given to works in English, though some important foreign titles are also
included. The reader will find that many of the books here
listed contain extensive bibliographies of their own which
will guide him in pursuit of more detailed study.

A. BOOKS

Barker, John W. *Manuel II Palaeologus, 1391–1425: A Study
in Late Byzantine Statesmanship*. New Brunswick, N. J.,
1969. An outstanding work of meticulous scholarship,
containing an excellent bibliography. Also includes
extensive translations from many of Manuel's letters
and other writings.

Bosch, Ursula V. *Andronikos III Palaiologos: Versuch einer*

Darstellung der byzantinischen Geschichte in den Jahren 1321–1341. Amsterdam, 1965. The first full-length volume devoted exclusively to Andronikos III. An important study.

Brand, Charles, ed. *Icon and Minaret: Sources of Byzantine and Islamic Civilization.* Englewood Cliffs, N. J., 1969. A "reader" of Byzantine source material; contains the anonymous eye-witness report of the Emperor Manuel's coronation.

Bréhier, Louis. *Le Monde byzantin.* 3 vols. Paris, 1947–1950. Lengthy coverage of political history is to be found in Vol. I, *Vie et mort de Byzance.* Later volumes offer valuable insights into institutional and cultural history.

The Cambridge Medieval History, vol. IV. Edited by Joan M. Hussey. Cambridge, 1966. Chapters on the Palaiologan period by D. M. Nicol and George Ostrogorsky. (Ostrogorsky's is almost identical with a chapter on the same era in his *History of the Byzantine State.*) *The Cambridge Medieval History* is indispensable to students of Byzantine history in all periods, with its comprehensive series of bibliographies.

Dennis, George T., S. J. *The Reign of Manuel II Palaeologus in Thessalonica, 1382–1387.* Orientalia Christiana Analecta, no. 159. Rome, 1960. An important and interesting monograph on Manuel's term as Despot of Thessaloniki. Contains numerous quotations from writings of Manuel and his associates.

Dereksen, David. *The Crescent and the Cross: The Fall of Byzantium. May 1453.* New York, 1964. A popularized account of the fall of Constantinople; lacks footnotes, but is generally accurate and based on good research.

Diehl, Charles. *Byzantine Empresses.* Translated by Harold Bell and Theresa de Kerpely. New York, 1963. Popularized but soundly researched biographical sketches by one of the greatest of modern Byzantinists. Contains chapters on Yolande of Montferrat and Anne of Savoy. The lack of any documentation is regrettable.

———— *Byzantium: Greatness and Decline.* Translated by

Naomi Walford. New Brunswick, N.J., 1957. A classic of Byzantine cultural history, also includes a lengthy and helpful bibliographical essay by Peter Charanis.

⸺. *Figures byzantines,* II ser. Paris, 1908. Original French version of some of the essays in *Byzantine Empresses,* also includes additional material on the late Palaiologoi.

Franzius, Enno. *History of the Byzantine Empire.* New York, 1967. A semipopular retelling of the whole Byzantine story from Constantine I through 1453. Borrows heavily from Ostrogorsky. Easy reading.

Gardner, Alice. *The Lascarids of Nicaea.* London, 1912, reprint Chicago, 1967. Although old, this volume continues to be a definitive work in English on the Byzantine Empire-in-exile.

Geanakoplos, Deno John. *Byzantine East and Latin West.* Oxford, 1966. A series of interpretative essays, including an interesting study on the Council of Florence.

⸺. *Emperor Michael Palaeologus and the West.* Cambridge, Mass., 1959. A classic of modern Byzantine scholarship, this work contains not only a detailed study of Michael VIII's foreign policy, but also considerable information on internal affairs during his reign. An extensive bibliography is included.

Gill, Joseph, S.J. *The Council of Florence.* Cambridge, England, 1959. Fully documented, detailed study; a definitive work on its subject.

⸺. *Personalities of the Council of Florence.* New York, 1964. By the recognized authority on the Council of Florence, this work contains short chapters on John VIII and other leading figures of the council.

Goodacre, Hugh. *A Handbook of the Coinage of the Byzantine Empire.* London, 1957. A standard work on Byzantine coinage, this volume also contains an interesting brief biographical sketch of each emperor.

Halecki, Oscar. *Un Empereur de Byzance à Rome: Vingt ans de travail pour l'Union des églises et pour la défence de l'empire d'orient, 1355–1373.* Warsaw, 1930. Though some minor points have been clarified by more recent research, Halecki's work still remains the definitive study on John V's negotiations with the Roman church.

Laiou, Angeliki E. *Constantinople and the Latins: The Foreign Policy of Andronicus II, 1282–1328.* Cambridge, Mass., 1972. Professor Laiou does for Andronikos II's reign what Geanakoplos has done for Michael VIII. An important, excellently documented work, destined to be the definitive study on this subject.

Lowe, Alfonso. *The Catalan Vengeance.* London, 1972. An entertaining yet well-researched retelling of the early adventures of the Catalan Grand Company from the pro-Catalan viewpoint.

Mijatovich, Chedomil. *Constantine Palaeologus: The Last Emperor of the Greeks, 1448–1453.* 1892, reprint Chicago, 1968. Not always reliable although beautifully written, this work must be used with caution. It is most valuable for extracts from the *Slavonic Chronicle*.

Miller, William. *Essays on the Latin Orient.* Amsterdam, 1964. Reprints of a number of important essays by a noted historian of the early twentieth century.

———. *The Latins in the Levant: A History of Frankish Greece (1204–1566).* London, 1908, reprint Cambridge, England, 1964. Justly considered a classic in the field of medieval Greek history, Miller's work concentrates on the Frankish principalities in Greece after the Fourth Crusade, but also contains valuable incidental information on the Palaiologoi, especially in the Morea.

Nicol, Donald M. *The Byzantine Family of Kantakouzenos (Cantacuzenus) ca. 1100–1460.* Washington, D.C., 1968. A wonderfully documented, scholarly study of the Kantakouzenos family and particularly of the career of the Emperor John VI.

———. *Byzantium: Its Ecclesiastical History and Relations with the Western World.* London, 1972. A series of scholarly essays including several on Palaiologan subjects reprinted from various learned journals.

———. *The Despotate of Epiros.* Oxford, 1957. A detailed

political history of the independent principality of Epiros in the thirteenth century and its struggles with the Laskarid Empire of Nicaea.

———— *The Last Centuries of Byzantium.* New York, 1972. An important survey of the Palaiologan period, with emphasis on political and military developments.

Ostrogorsky, George. *History of the Byzantine State.* Revised edition. Translated by Joan M. Hussey. Oxford, 1968. Unquestionably the best textbook of Byzantine history available to the English reader. A classic of scholarship.

Ostroumoff, Ivan N. *The History of the Council of Florence.* Translated by Basil Popoff. Boston, 1971. Interesting for what it is, a highly partisan work denouncing the "unionizers" and John VIII and lauding Bishop Mark Eugenikos of Ephesus.

Papadopulos, Averikos Th. *Versuch einer Genealogie der Palaiologen, 1259–1453.* Munich, 1938, reprint Amsterdam, 1962. The basic genealogical study of the Palaiologoi; includes a very helpful and detailed "family tree" chart.

Parisot, Valentin. *Cantacuzène, homme d'état et historien.* Paris, 1845. Although over a century old, Parisot's study is still one of the most thorough presentations of the career and literary undertakings of Kantakouzenos.

Pears, Edwin. *The Destruction of the Greek Empire and the Story of the Capture of Constantinople by the Turks.* 1903, reprint New York, 1968. For many years considered the "standard" work on the fall of Constantinople, Pears' volume is still useful although somewhat superseded by more modern research.

Polemis, Demetrios I. *The Doukai: A Contribution to Byzantine Prosopography.* London, 1968. A scholarly study of the Doukas families in Byzantine history, with many interesting incidental biographical details included.

Runciman, Sir Steven. *The Fall of Constantinople, 1453.* Cambridge, England, 1969. Unbiased and written in a pleasantly readable style, this volume unfortunately also contains some rather serious factual errors and must be used with caution.

_____. *The Sicilian Vespers*. Cambridge, England, 1958. A vivid and highly readable account of the international politics in the Mediterranean world in the late thirteenth century, including the schemes of Michael VIII.

Setton, Kenneth Meyer. *The Catalan Domination of Athens, 1311–1388*. Cambridge, Mass., 1948. The classic study of the subject, extensively documented.

Sherrard, Philip. *Byzantium*. ("Great Ages of Man: Time-Life Books"). New York, 1966. A lavishly illustrated, well-written introduction to the Byzantine world.

Vacalopoulos, Apostolos E. *Origins of the Greek Nation: The Byzantine Period, 1207–1461*. Translated by Ian Moles. New Brunswick, N. J., 1970. Interesting emphasis on intellectual history.

Vasiliev, Alexander A. *History of the Byzantine Empire*. Madison, Wisconsin, 1958. A pioneering work in Byzantine studies; somewhat superseded by Ostrogorsky but still useful.

Vryonis, Speros. *The Decline of Medieval Hellenism in Asia Minor and the Process of Islamization from the Eleventh through the Fifteenth Century*. Berkeley, 1971. A monumental work, detailed and extensively documented, on social, intellectual, and religious changes accompanying the gradual Turkish conquest of Byzantine territory.

Whitting, Philip, editor. *Byzantium: An Introduction*. New York, 1971. A deceptively simple survey of Byzantine history in a series of essays by outstanding scholars; the chapter on the Palaiologoi is by Father Joseph Gill.

B. SHORTER MONOGRAPHS AND ARTICLES

Barker, John W. "John VII in Genoa: A Problem in Late Byzantine Source Confusion." *Orientalia Christiana Periodica* 28 (1962), 213–238.

———. "On the Chronology of the Activities of Manuel II Palaeologus in the Morea in 1415." *Byzantinische Zeitschrift* 55 (1962), 39–55.

———. "The Problem of Appanages in Byzantium during the Palaiologan Period." *Byzantina* 3 (1971), 105–122.

Brightman, F. E. "Byzantine Imperial Coronations." *Journal of Theological Studies* 2 (1901), 359–392.

Carroll, Margaret. "Notes on the Authorship of the 'Siege' Section of the *Chronicon Maius* of Pseudo-Phrantzes, Book III." *Byzantion* 41 (1971), 28–44.

Charanis, Peter. "The Strife among the Palaeologi and the Ottoman Turks, 1370–1402." *Byzantion* 16 (1942–43), 286–315.

Chrysostomides, Julian. "John V Palaeologus in Venice (1370–71), and the Chronicle of Caroldo: a Reinterpretation." *Orientalia Christiana Periodica* 31 (1965), 76–84.

Dennis, George T. "An Unknown Byzantine Emperor: Andronicus V Palaeologus (1400–1407?)." *Jahrbuch der Österreichischen Gesselschaft* 16 (1967), 175–187.

Diehl, Charles. "L'Empire byzantin sous les Paléologues." *Études Byzantines.* Paris, 1905, reprint, New York, 1963.

Dölger, Franz. "Johannes VII, Kaiser der Rhomäer, 1390–1408." *Byzantinische Zeitschrift* 31 (1931), 21–36.

Halecki, Oscar. "Two Palaeologi in Venice, 1370–71." *Byzantion* 17 (1944–45), 331–335.

Jugie, M. "Le Voyage de l'empereur Manuel Paléologue en Occident (1399–1403)." *Échos d'Orient* 15 (1912), 322–332.

Kolias, G. "Constantin Paléologue, le dernier défenseur de Constantinople." *L'Hellénisme contemporain* (Athens, 1953), 41–54.

Laiou, Angeliki E. "A Byzantine Prince Latinized: Theodore Palaeologus, Marquis of Montferrat." *Byzantion* 38 (1968), 386–410.

Loenertz, Raymond-J. "Autour de *Chronicon Maius* attribué à Georges Phrantzes." *Miscellanea G. Mercati* 3 *Letteratura e storia bizantina* (Studi e Testi, 123; Rome, 1946), 273–311.

————. "Une erreur singulière de Laonic Chalcocandyle: Le prétendu second mariage de Jean V Paléologue," *Revue des études byzantines* 15 (1957), 176–184.

————. "Jean V Paléologue à Venise (1370–1371)." *Revue des études byzantines* 16 (1958), 217–232.

————. "La Première insurrection d'Andronic IV Paléologue." *Échos d'Orient* 38 (1939), 334–345.

Luke, H. C. "Visitors from the East to the Plantagenet and Lancastrian Kings." *Nineteenth Century* 108 (1930), 760-769.

Marinesco, Constantin. "Deux empereurs byzantins, Manuel II et Jean VIII Paléologue, vus par des artistes occidentaux." *Le Flambeau* 40 (Nov.-Dec. 1957), 758–762.

Megas, G. "La Prise de Constantinople dans la poésie et la tradition populaires grecques." *"L'Hellénisme contemporain* (Athens, 1953), 125–133.

Meyendorf, Jean. "Projets de Concile oecuménique en 1367: Un dialogue inedit entre Jean Cantacuzène et le légat Paul." *Dumbarton Oaks Papers* 14 (1960), 149–177.

Nicol, Donald M. "The Abdication of John Cantacuzene." *Byzantinische Forschungen* 2 (Amsterdam, 1967), 269–283.

Papadrianos, Ioannis A. "The Marriage Arrangement between Constantine XI Palaeologus and the Serbian Mara (1451)." *Balkan Studies* 6 (1965), 131–138.

Schlumberger, Gustave. "Un Empereur de Byzance à Paris et à Londres." *Byzance et Croisades*. Paris, 1927, 87–147.

Ševčenko, Ihor. "The Decline of Byzantium Seen Through the Eyes of Its Intellectuals." *Dumbarton Oaks Papers* 15 (1961), 169– 186.

Vasiliev, Alexander A. "La Guerre de cent ans et Jeanne d'Arc dans la tradition byzantine." *Byzantion* 3 (1926), 241–250.

————. "Pero Tafur: A Spanish Traveler of the Fifteenth Century and His Visit to Constantinople, Trebizond, and Italy." *Byzantion* 7 (1932), 75–122.

Index

199

CONSTANCE HEAD is a professor of history at Western Carolina University in Cullowhee, North Carolina, where she has taught since 1967 and where her areas of specialization include Roman and Byzantine studies. She received undergraduate and graduate degrees from Duke University, Durham, North Carolina.

Dr. Head is the author of two other books, *Justinian II of Byzantium* and *The Emperor Julian*, and a number of scholarly articles which have appeared in *Byzantion*, *Archivum Historiae Pontificiae*, and the *Catholic Historical Review*. She also has written several popular history studies published in periodicals such as *Mankind* and *History Today*.